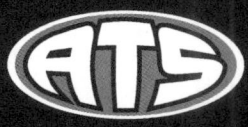

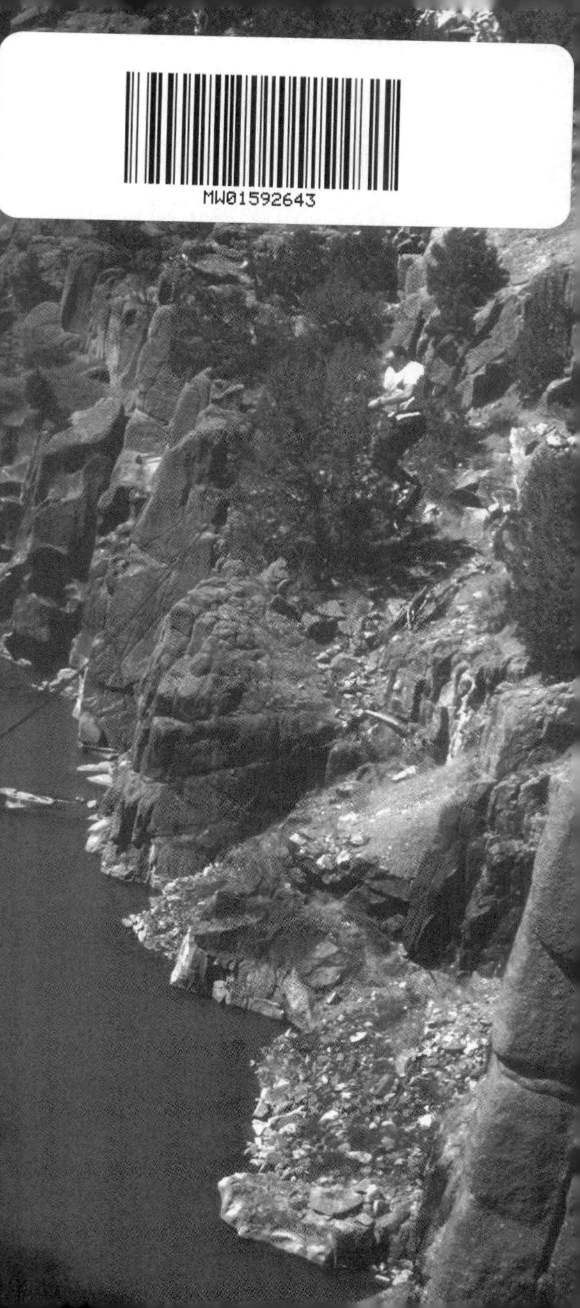

"Needles" going big in Fremont Canyon, Wyoming.

Warning! Read this before using this book.

Climbing is an inherently dangerous sport in which severe injuries or death may occur. Relying on the information in this book may increase the danger.

When climbing you can only rely on your skill, training, experience and conditioning. **If you have any doubts as to your ability to safely climb any route in this guide, do not try it.**

This book is neither a professional climbing instructor nor a substitute for one. **It is not an instructional book. Do not use it as one.** It contains information that is nothing more than a compilation of opinions about climbing the boulder problems of Vedauwoo. **Those opinions are neither facts nor promises.** Treat the information as opinions and nothing more. Do not substitute these opinions for your own common sense and experience.

Assumption of Risk
There may be errors in this book resulting from the inadvertent mistakes of the authors and/or the people with whom they consulted. The information was gathered from a variety of sources, which may not have been independently verified. Those who provided the information may have made mistakes in their descriptions. The authors may have made mistakes in their conveyance of the information in this book. **They cannot, therefore, guarantee the correctness of any of the information contained in the book.** The topographical maps, the photo-diagrams, the difficulty ratings , the protection ratings, the approach and/or descending information, the suggestions about equipment and other matters may be incorrect or misleading. Fixed protection may not be where indicated, may be absent, or may be unreliable. **You must keep in mind that the information in this book may be erroneous and use your own judgement when choosing, approaching, climbing or descending from a route described in this book.**

Do not use this book unless you assume the risk of its errors of reportage of judgement and of its other defects.

Disclaimer of Warranties
The authors and publisher warn that this book contains only the authors' opinion on the subjects discussed. They make no other warranties, expressed or implied, of the merchantability, fitness for purpose, or otherwise, and in any event, their liability for breach of any warranty or contract with respect to the content of this book is limited to the purchase price of the book. They further limit such purchase price their liability on account of any kind of negligent behavior whatsoever on their part with respect to the contents of this book.

Opposite Photo: Davin Bagdonas

VEDAUWOO BOULDERING

Davin Bagdonas

Extreme Angles Publishing

**Published by
Extreme Angles
PO Box 973
Laramie, WY 82072
www.extremeangles.com**

Cover Illustration: Rachael Lynn

Cover Photo Credits Clockwise: Clint Cook on Broken China by Davin Bagdonas, Sky at Central by Rachael Lynn, Erik Christensen on Suzuki Roof by Josh Helke, Trevor Turmelle on Good Vibrations by Josh Helke, Pad People by Josh Helke, Liz Hajek on Desperado by Josh Helke

Maps and layout by Extreme Angles.

Opposite: Alex McKiernan on Scared Money Can't Win, Citadel. Photo: Davin Bagdonas

Table of Contents

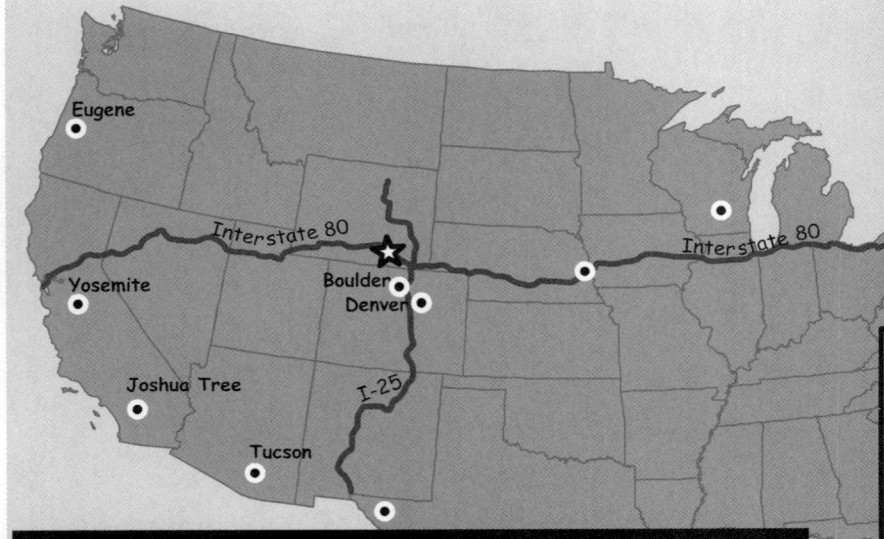

From	Driving Time	Miles
Tucson, Arizona	16 Hours	1060
Joshua Tree, California	17.5 Hours	1020
Yosemite NP, California	18 Hours	1100
Asheville, North Carolina	23.5 Hours	1500
Boulder, Colorado	2 Hours	115
Denver, Colorado	2 Hours	125
Omaha, Nebraska	8 Hours	525
NYC, New York	27 Hours	1760
Shawanagunks, New York	27 Hours	1780
Eugene, Oregon	18.5 Hours	1250
Hueco Tanks, Texas	12.5 Hours	840
Madison, Wisconsin	15 Hours	950

At a Glance

How to get to Vedauwoo

Vedauwoo is located right off Interstate 80, just 40 miles West of Interstate 25 and Cheyenne. Use exit 329 to reach Vedauwoo Road and the Central areas, and use exit 323 to access Happy Jack Road areas.

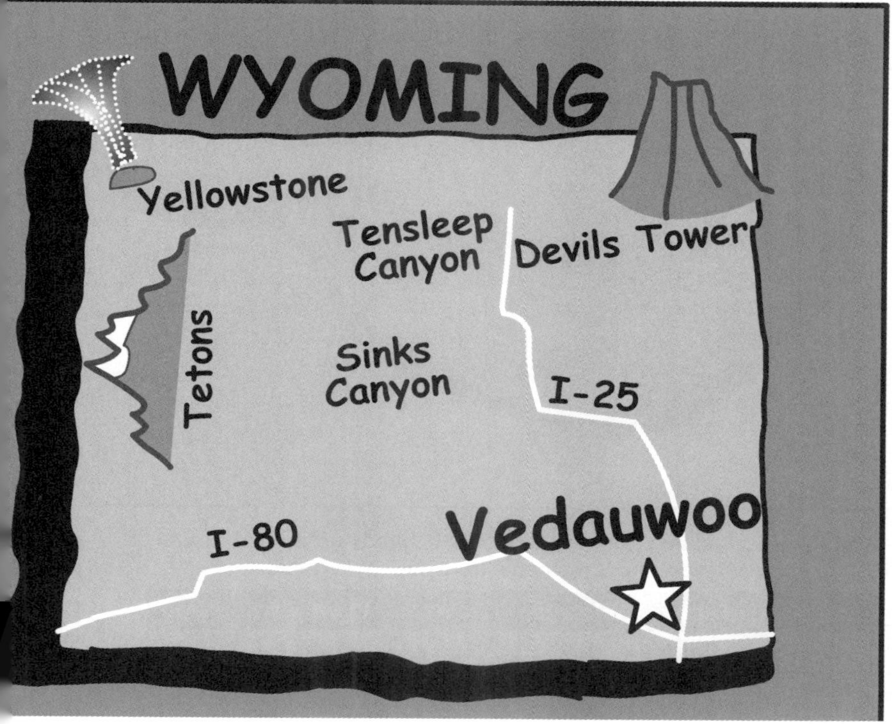

Shawanagunks

New York City

At a Glance

WYOMING

Yellowstone

Tensleep Canyon

Devils Tower

Tetons

Sinks Canyon

I-25

I-80

Vedauwoo

Geographical Table of Contents

The following tables are a quick reference guide to each specific bouldering area. Use them to navigate throughout the book and throughout Vedauwoo.

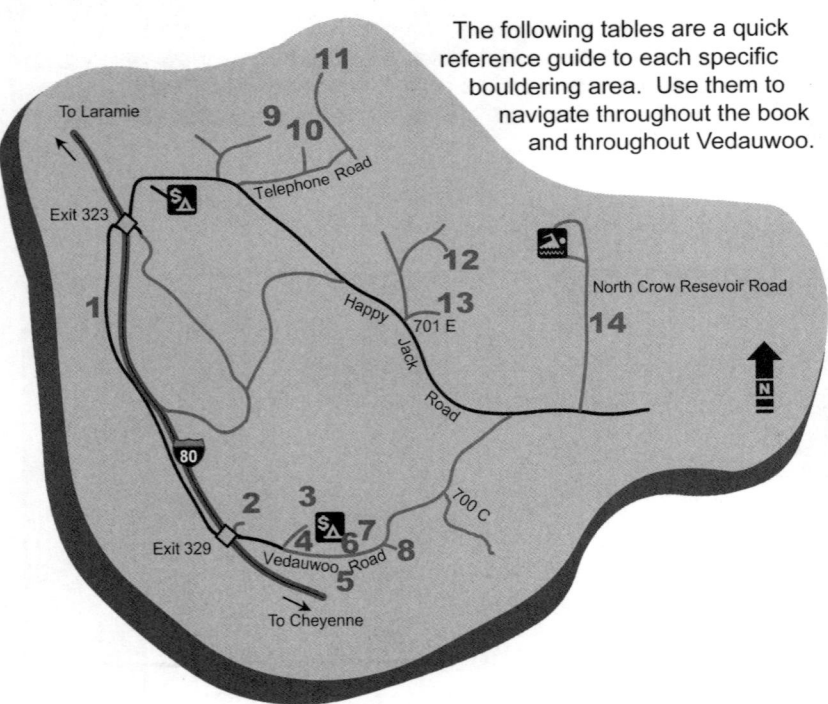

This table is calculated from exit 323 of I-80, heading South on Route 30. Mileage and turns begin from the cattle guard.

	Area Name	Mileage	Turns*	Problems	Page
1	School Yard	1.4	2nd Right	46	19

*From exit 323 head South on route 30. Mileage starts at cattle guard.

This table is calculated from exit 329 of I-80, heading East on Vedauwoo Road. Mileage and turns start from the second cattle guard.

	Area Name	Mileage	Turns*	Problems	Page
2	Bistro	NA	1st left	23	34
3	Central	NA	2nd Left	117	62

*From exit 329 head East on Vedauwoo Road. Mileage and turns start from the second cattle guard.

This table is calculated from exit 329 of I-80, heading East on Vedauwoo Road. Mileage and turns start from where Vedauwoo Road turns to dirt.

	Area Name	Mileage	Turns*	Problems	Page
4	Nautilus	0.2	1st Left	71	42
5	Nat's	0.6	1st Right	30	91
6	Dirty Deeds	1.3	6th Left	6	99
7	Moon/Alice	1.8	11th Left	2	103
8	Citadel	2	5th Right	101	105

*From exit 329 head East on Vedauwoo Road. Mileage and turns start from where Vedauwoo Road turns to dirt.

This table is calculated from exit 323 onto Happy Jack road. Mileage and turns begin when you turn on to Happy Jack Road.

	Area Name	Mileage	Turns*	Problems	Page
9	Coyote Rocks	2.3	2nd Left	45	141
10	Telephone Road	2.75	3rd Left	29	155
11	Eagle Rocks	2.75	4th Left	49	165
12	Bunker	7.7	4th Left	48	179
13	Roof Ranch	7.7	4th Left	35	191
14	Campjack Rocks	12	7th Left	40	206

*From exit 323 turn on to Happy Jack road. Mileage and turns begin when you turn on to Happy Jack Road.

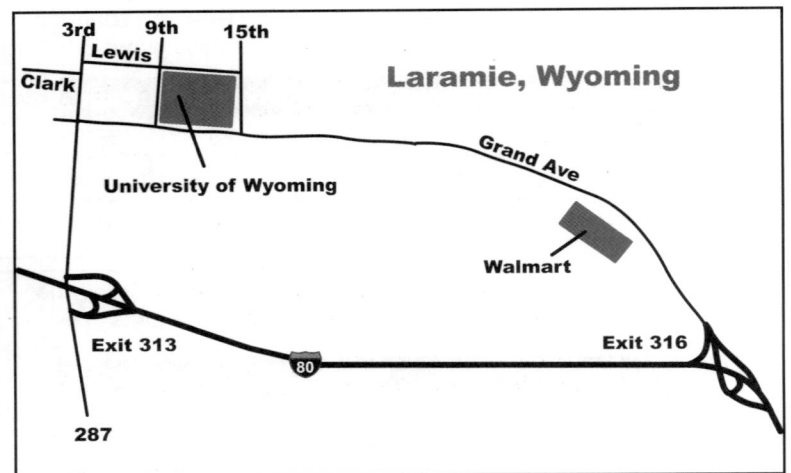

Laramie Eats, Treats and Sheets

Camping
Vedauwoo is located in the Medicine Bow National Forest; therefore campers must abide by National Forest regulations. Basically, camping is free outside designated campgrounds. Refrain from "creating" new campsites and use common sense to locate areas that have already been used in order to limit your impact.

Eats:
For coffee in the morning, check out Coal Creek Coffee between 1st and 2nd, or Grounds on 3rd St. By far, the Chuckwagon has the best breakfasts in town. Their Cowhand Special is huge and cheap. They also serve beer if you stop by later in the day. They are located just off 80 at exit 313. Right across the street you will find Corona Village for $4 all you can eat tacos every Tuesday night.

Internet/Atm
The University of Wyoming's Student Union has numerous computer

workstations available, none of which are password restrictive. ATM machines are located at the East entrance of the building. Also be sure to check out the campus calendar for any events. Grounds Lounge and E-bar on 3rd Street also has free internet access and excellent coffee.

Entertainment

Mingles has free pool 3-6 daily and all day Sunday. They are located just off Grand Ave. right next to Albertson's. They also have a drive-up window. You can catch a flick at the Fox Cinema on 505 South 20th, or the cheap seats of the Wyo Theatre on 309 South 5th.

Mountain Shops

All Terrain Sports, Atmosphere, Big Hoss Mountain Sports and Cross Country Connection will have what you need for supplementing your rack. Atmosphere will also do custom design work or patch up any worn-out packs or tents. Check out the shops when you're in town.

Sheets

The Travel Inn Motel on 3rd St. and Snowy Range Road offer the cheapest rates in town, DSL in your room and a swimming pool in the summer.

Rest Days

Too gnarled to climb? Raspberries getting infected? Partner starting to annoy you at the crags? Well, you're in luck because you are in adventure country and there is lots to do in the Laramie area.

Hiking, Skiing, Alpine

The Snowy Range, just a half hour drive from Laramie, offers a wealth of hiking and mountain bike trails. The Snowies, as they are known, are steep, rugged and heavily treed. In the spring (yes, May counts) there are still snow fields in which many squeeze ten to twenty turns or practice self-arrest techniques. Another rest day activity is a hike to the summit of Medicine Bow Peak (12,013 feet). The view from the top is incredible; just be sure to watch out for afternoon lightning storms.

Whitewater Rafting and Kayaking

River running on Colorado's North Platte from Route to 6-Mile thrashes in at a class III/IV. It is roughly 9.8 miles and will take 3-4 hours. For guide info contact www.hpoiadventure.com.

Skateboarding

Bring your skateboard and check out Laramie's concrete skate park at 5th Street and Canby in Labonte Park.

Mountain Biking

Great mountain biking can be had on the Happy Jack Trails by the Lincoln Head. Go to ExtremeAngles.com to download trail info and elevation profiles.

Caving

For those interested in 3-D bouldering, check out some of Wyoming's caves. One cave is within 3 hours of Laramie. For info, check out Wayne Sutherland's *Caves of Wyoming*, which is available for purchase at the Wyoming Geological Survey Building on the campus of the University of Wyoming.

Swimming and Cliff Jumping

For swimming and cliff jumping, head over to Curt Gowdy Reservoir. There are beaches to hang out on and many different fingers of the reservoir to be explored.

Hot Springs

The Saratoga Hot Springs are located in the small town of Saratoga, Wyoming on the western side of the Snowies. For some great rest day relaxation, make the trek. They are free and worth the drive.

Opposite: Liz Hajek slogs through the snow
Photo: Josh Helke

Weather:

Vedauwoo is not for sissies. In addition to sharp rock and high winds, the Wyoming weather can often test the most committed of boulderers. The best weather can usually be found between May and September, but there are times even in the cold months when the sun comes out and sheltered areas can be quite balmy.

HELP STOP OFFROAD VEHICLE DAMAGE ON PUBLIC LANDS ★ CONTACT THE FOREST SERVICE/ BLM IN YOUR AREA.

THIS AD SPONSORED BY CCH – ALIENS
115 LYON STREET, LARAMIE, WY 82072
307.721.9385 ★ EMAIL: CCHALIENS@AOL.COM

Trevor Turmelle searching for Little America, V5 at
Campjack Rocks.
Photo: Davin Bagdonas.

**Opposite: Matt Williams on Problem 11, V4 at the School Yard.
Photo: Davin Bagdonas.**

18

School Yard

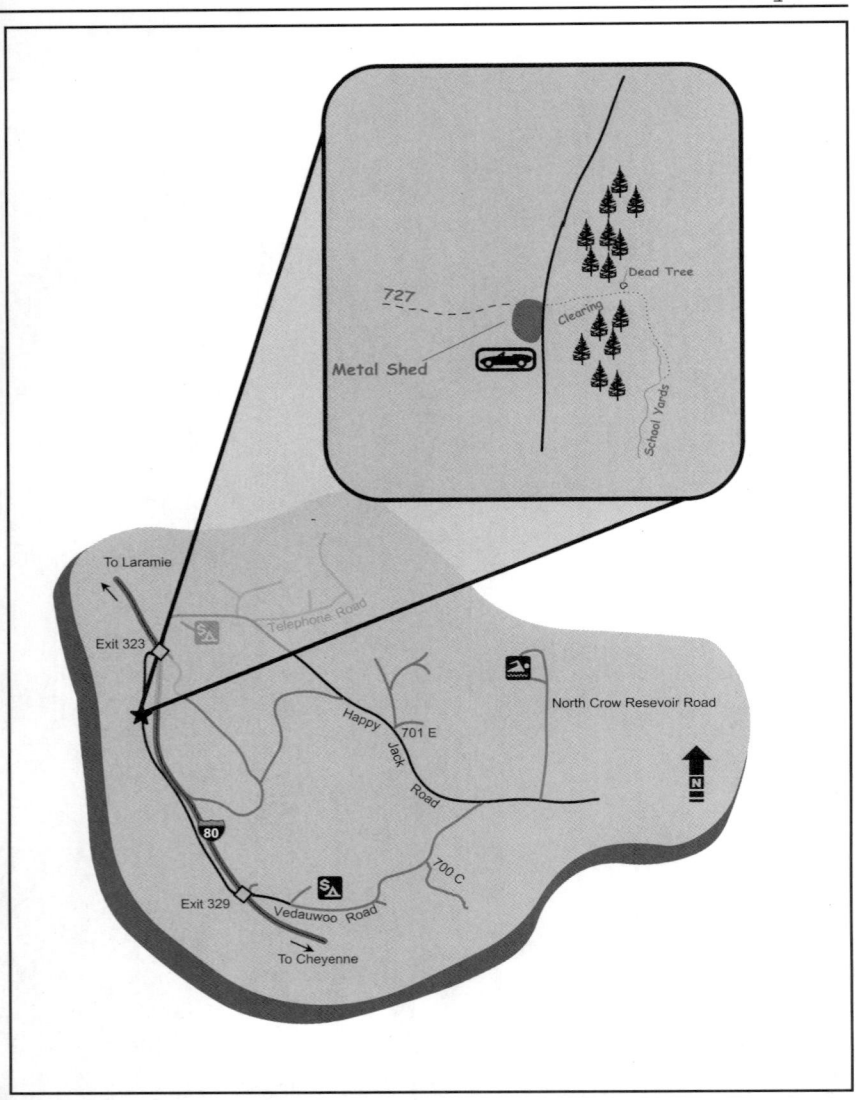

School Yard

	Area Name	Mileage	Turns*
1	School Yard	1.4	2nd Right

*From exit 323 head South on route 30. Mileage starts at cattle guard.

Directions

From I-80, take the Happy Jack exit and head west (away from the rest area) on Highway 30. Drive along the curving road for 1.4 miles to a gravel pit on the right. Park at this parking lot away from any machinery, or further down Forest Service road 727. From the parking lot, walk east across the paved road into the open sagebrush prairie. Head toward a prominent dead tree on the horizon. At the tree, hike down the gully to the cliffs on your right.

Problem Distribution Table

	V0-V3	V4-V7	V8-V10	V11+	Cracks	Total*
Quantity	31	12	1	0	2	46

*Total includes projects and unrated problems.

Following pages: Davin Bagdonas on Problem 10, V3, while Dave Nash looks on.
Photo: Matt Williams

School Yard

South School Yard

1. V3
This is the southern most problem at the School Yard. It is short and goes up a technical, vertical face on a small boulder below the cliff band.

2. V1
This is the short face banded with pink and white.

3. V2
Climb through the bulge on slopers and edges.

4. V3
On the left end of the wall in the corridor, on the boulder that holds the previous problem, climb this V3 using grey colored slopers.

5. V0
Climb the slab up between the bushes growing from cracks.

6. V0
Climb the slab.

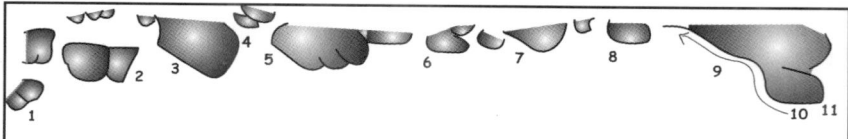

7. V2
Blocky start up the blunt prow on edges.

8. V3
Use slopers and edges up the vertical face. This problem is on a separate boulder just to the left of the wide, featured face.

9. V1
Good traversing moves on the featured face. Start on the detached boulder's arete on the right end of the wall. Go around the detached boulder, span to the wide, featured wall and go till the rock runs out.

10. V4
Sit start the vertical face of the detached block.

11. V5
Sit start the overhanging prow of the detached block.

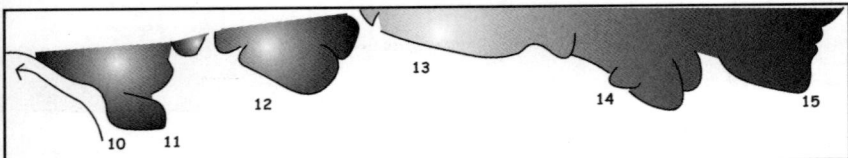

12. V1
Climb the tall slab on sloping edges, right of the gash-looking seams. Located on the tall striped wall.

13. V0
Short slab problem that is less steep and shorter than the previous slab problem.

14. V2
Start low on the pillar that sits on the right end of the broken and overgrown wall. Slap up the pillar avoiding rock on either side.

15. V1
This is the last sizable wall of the South School Yard when walking north along the walls. Climb the blunt prow on broken looking rock.

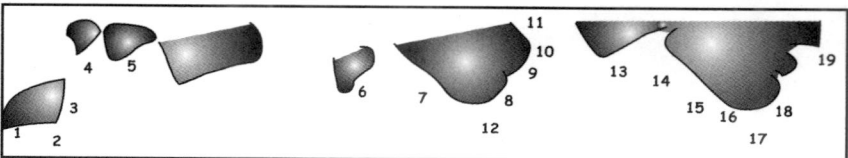

Middle School Yard

1. V2
This problem is the southern-most problem in the Middle School Yard. Dyno from the low, sloping edge to the lip of the boulder.

2. V2
Sit start the blunt prow of the boulder.

3. V4
Climb slopers up the just past vertical face of the boulder that holds the two previous problems.

4. V4
Low start on the less-than-vertical bulge, using slopers. Top out with a sloping mantle.

5. V0
Climb the pink face then step right to the arete and continue on crumbly rock.

6. V2
Dyno or dead point to the lip of the boulder from the sloping dish.

Matt Williams on Problem 16.
Photo: Davin Bagdonas.

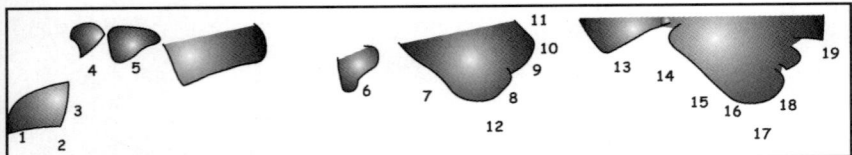

7. V8
Black face on left side of the boulder. Sit start on edges, right heel hook then follow slopers and crimps.

8. V5
Sit start the roof on the good pinch/edge, go to the sloper at the lip at the bottom of the seam, and climb left on slopers. This problem mantles left of the vertical seam and grass tuffs.

9. V3
Sit start on crisp edges just right of the overhang (broken looking rock). Big moves gain the lip of the boulder.

10. V3
Low start, in the overhang, just right of the previous problem. Use good edges and breaks up the vertical face.

11. V4
Sit start on the white sloping edge, on the right, uphill end of the boulder. Go up using sloping crimpers to gain the lip at the juniper tree.

12. Traverse V5
Start on problem 8 and go right at the lip of the roof. Finish by doing problem 11.

13. V6
Right to left lip traverse that ends with a sloping mantle.

School Yard

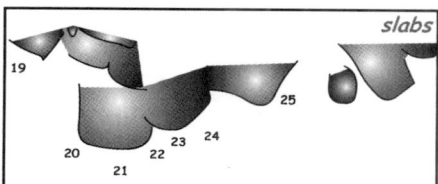

slabs

14. V2
This is the left-most problem on the wall with the wide diagonal crack. Start on sloping rails on the left end of the wall and go up.

15. V3
Low edge start to the dark streaked, sloping pinch. Up on sloping edges.

16. V2/3
Start low on the bottom of the diagonal wide crack on slopers. Slap up the gash using perfect slopers and not so good feet. Reach up to the broken looking pocket and top out. This is a really good problem!

17. V3
Boulder the face, just right of the diagonal gash and left of the bush that grows out of the face higher up.

18. V0
Climb the right side of the concave scoop.

19. V1
This is the slabby pink face uphill from the previous problem. The landing is a bit tilted.

20. V2
Climb the left-leaning, broken looking arete that divides the slab from the overhang.

21. V2/3
Traverse the slab and overhanging face by starting on problem 22 and climbing through the previous problem. Finish on the far end of the overhanging face.

22. V3
Sit start the right-leaning prow. Climb up without turning the prow to the left. A nice little toss for the incut edge finishes this problem.

23. V5
This is the vertical face just right of the previous problem. It uses technical crimps and the prow on the left to set up for the toss to the lip of the face.

24. V4
Sit start the overhanging prow of the boulder on the low, sloping edge. A bad heel scum and body tension allow you to reach the sloping edges up higher.

25. Project V?
The overhanging face in the corridor uphill and right of the previous problem.

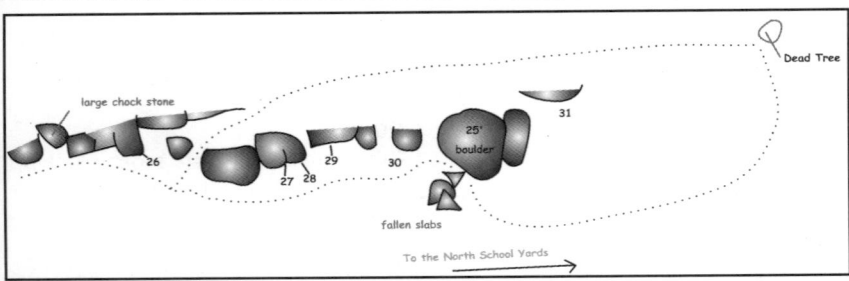

large chock stone

26

27 28

29

30

25' boulder

31

fallen slabs

Dead Tree

To the North School Yards

26. V4
Climb the tall overhanging arete with a step in the middle.
27. 5.10+
Off width to finger crack.
28. 5.11-
Sit start the finger and thin hands crack.
29. V2
This is the short roof problem on the wall just right and uphill from the previous crack problems.
30. V4
Climb sloping rails up the left side of the of the orange lichen covered wall, just above the fallen slabs.
31. V1-V3
Various roof problems on the wall above the big boulder. These are the last problems on the north end the Middle School Yard.

Opposite: Davin Bagdonas on Problem 11 Photo: Matt Williams.

26

30

27 28

29

31

Bistro Boulders

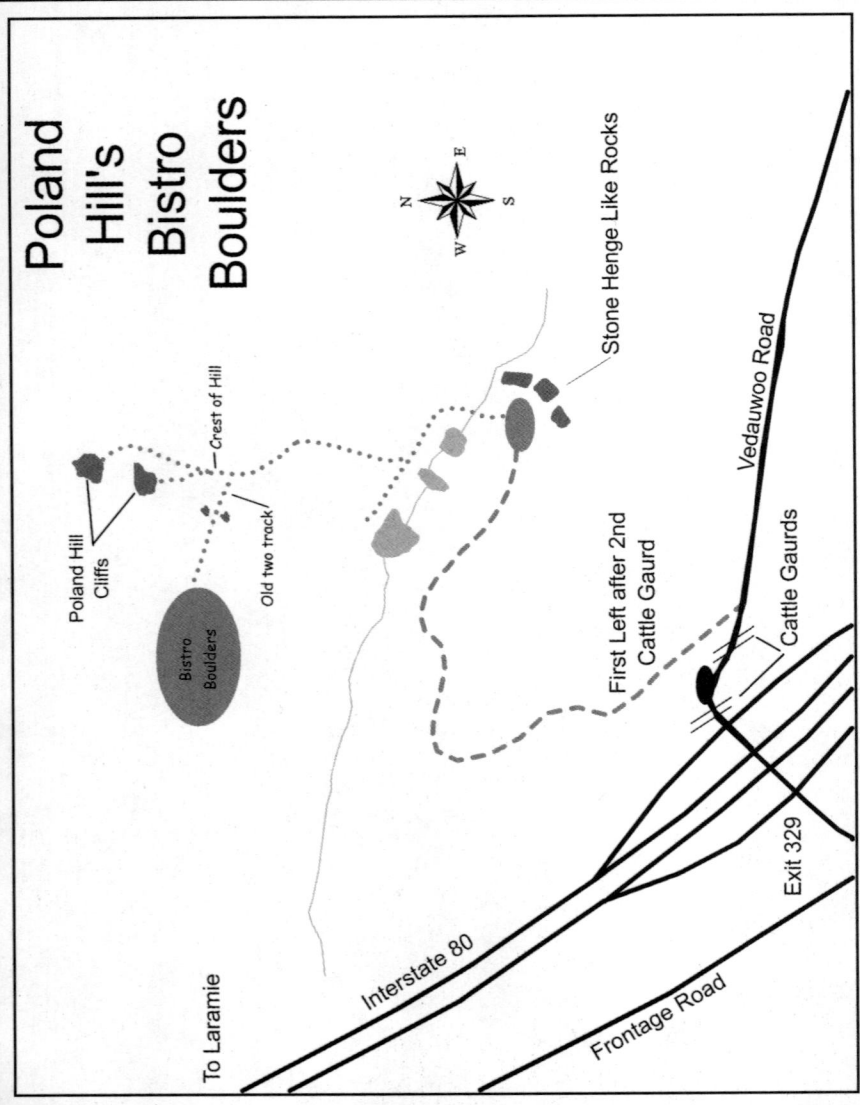

Poland Hill's Bistro Boulders

Stone Henge Like Rocks

Poland Hill Cliffs

Crest of Hill

Old two track

Bistro Boulders

Vedauwoo Road

First Left after 2nd Cattle Gaurd

Cattle Gaurds

Exit 329

Interstate 80

Frontage Road

To Laramie

Bistro Boulders

	Area Name	Mileage	Turns*
2	Bistro	NA	1st left

*From exit 329 head East on Vedauwoo Road. Mileage and turns start from the second cattle guard.

Directions

From I-80, take Vedauwoo Exit (329) to Vedauwoo Road. Hang a left after crossing two cattle guards, onto Forest Service road 700G. Follow this road until it ends at the Stone Henge looking rocks. From the parking lot, follow a trail that leads north. Cross the stream and continue following the trail up the hill. Just before the crest of the hill, head left on an old two-track road. Follow the road until you see slabs on your right. At this point, head left toward a prominent cone in the distance.

Problem Distribution Table

	V0-V3	V4-V7	V8-V10	V11+	Cracks	Total
Quantity	8	1	0	0	12	23

*Total includes projects and unrated problems.

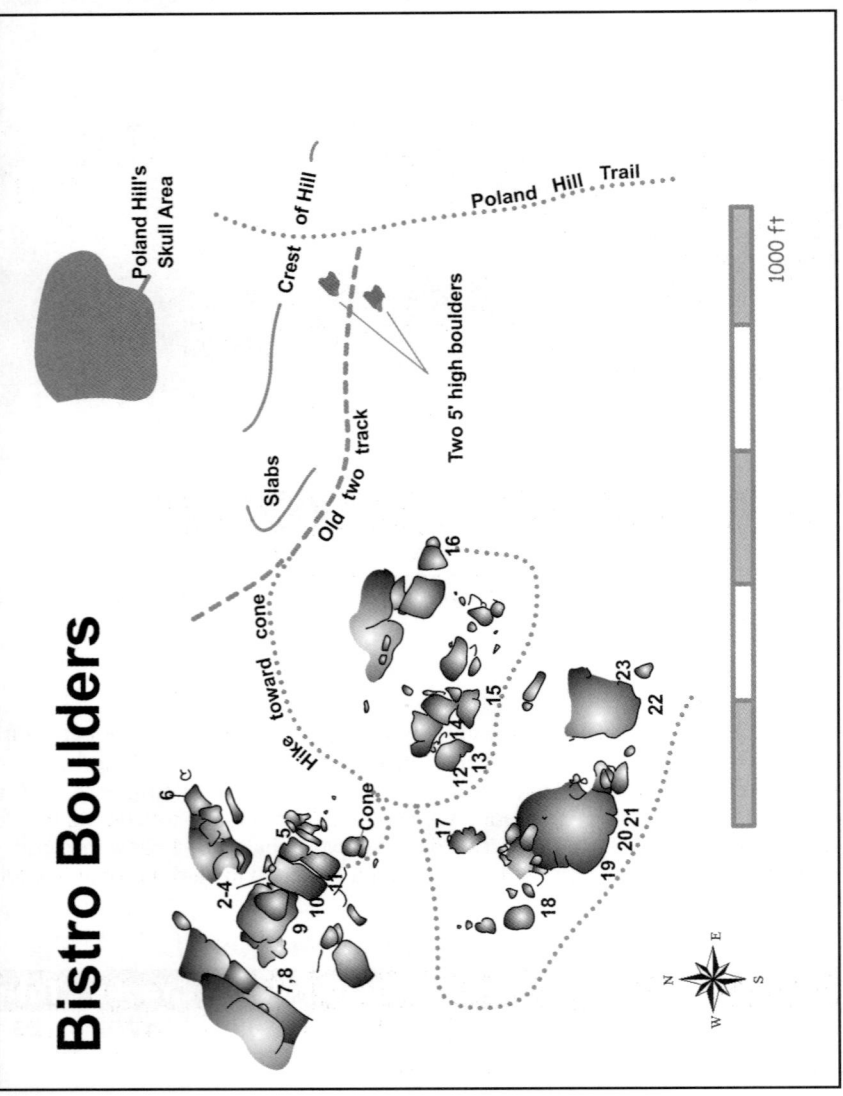

Bistro Boulders

1. Slam Dunk V0
Located on the back of the center boulder in the Parking Area. A fun dyno to a loose basketball sized cobble. Top out by moving left for the crack.
2. 5.10
Climb the wide crack that is back in the chimney.
3. 5.9
Sit start the hand crack in the chimney.
4. Happy V1
Follow really good edges up the arete
5. Project (The Bolrog)
This project follows crimps up the gentle overhang of the prow.
6. Lichen Burn 5.11
Harder than it looks but not even close to good. Sit start the short hand and fist crack in the small roof facing Poland Hill.
7. Zachary Slab V0
Climb the tallest part of the slab using a diagonal seam and jug half way up.

Bistro Boulders

8. Lego Man V0
This traverse starts on the sloping holds of a short seam on the left end of the wall above some ground juniper. Move right through and finish on the previous problem.

9. Come Original V6
Sit start this problem with the right hand on the semi-good lip and a good foot. Slap up the prow.

10. Classically Getting Wider 5.11
Sit start the hand crack corner. It turns into an off width higher up.

11. Length Not Girth 5.10
The tall hand to shaky fist crack.

12. V2
Sit start the diagonal flakes.

13. V0
Sit start up a shallow flared corner.

14. 5.10
Sit start hand crack and flake. 5.9 if started standing.

15. 5.12?
Finger crack roof that is topped with an awkward, hard finish at the roof's lip.

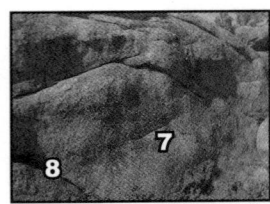

16. Spider Tooth Circus Trick 5.12-
A wide roof crack where two boulders meet. Start on hand jams and work through the wide crack in the middle.
17. Crumbly Corner V2
Climb the disintegrating corner.
18. Project
On the large boulder just left of the Bistro Wall, in the aspen grove. Follow the inclusions around to the lip of the boulder and mantle.
19. Bistro Left 5.12
Start in a roof dihedral and climb the crack around a corner. Finish on insecure moves up top.
20. The Bistro 5.11
Classic crack problem through the middle of the Bistro Wall.
21. Poise Colorado 5.11
This is the right-most crack on the Bistro Wall. Start with awkward moves in the roof to gain purchase on the crack above.
22. Truckers Corner V3
Lieback corner and finish on the slab.
23. Trucker's Flair 5.6
Climb the left leaning, flared hand crack. There is a bush growing in the bottom of this crack.

Bistro Boulders

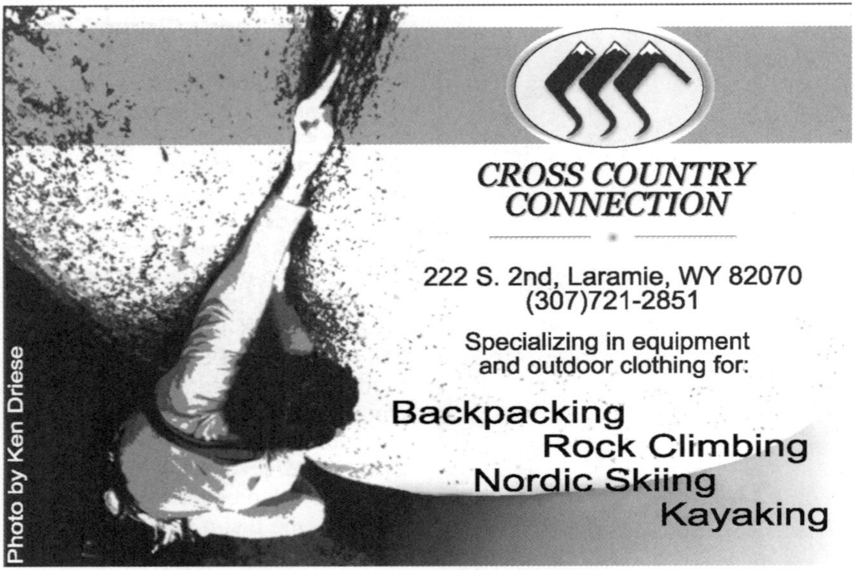

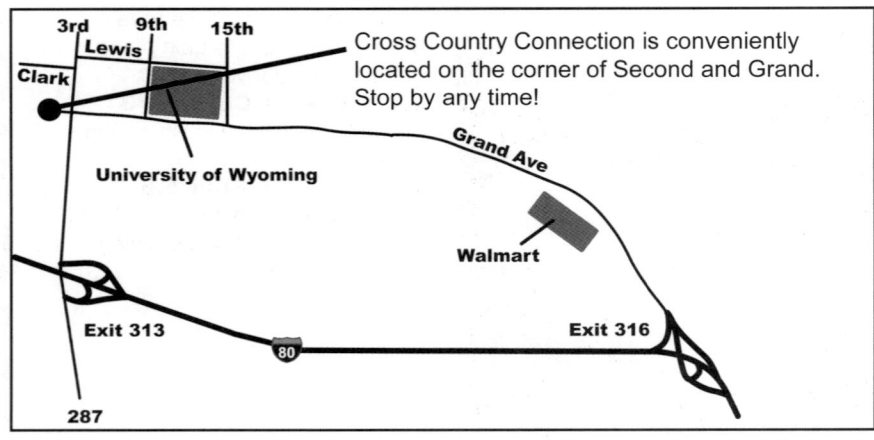
Opposite: Steve Millard on Sun Up Till Sundown.
Photo: Ken Driese.

Nautilus

Nautilus Boulders

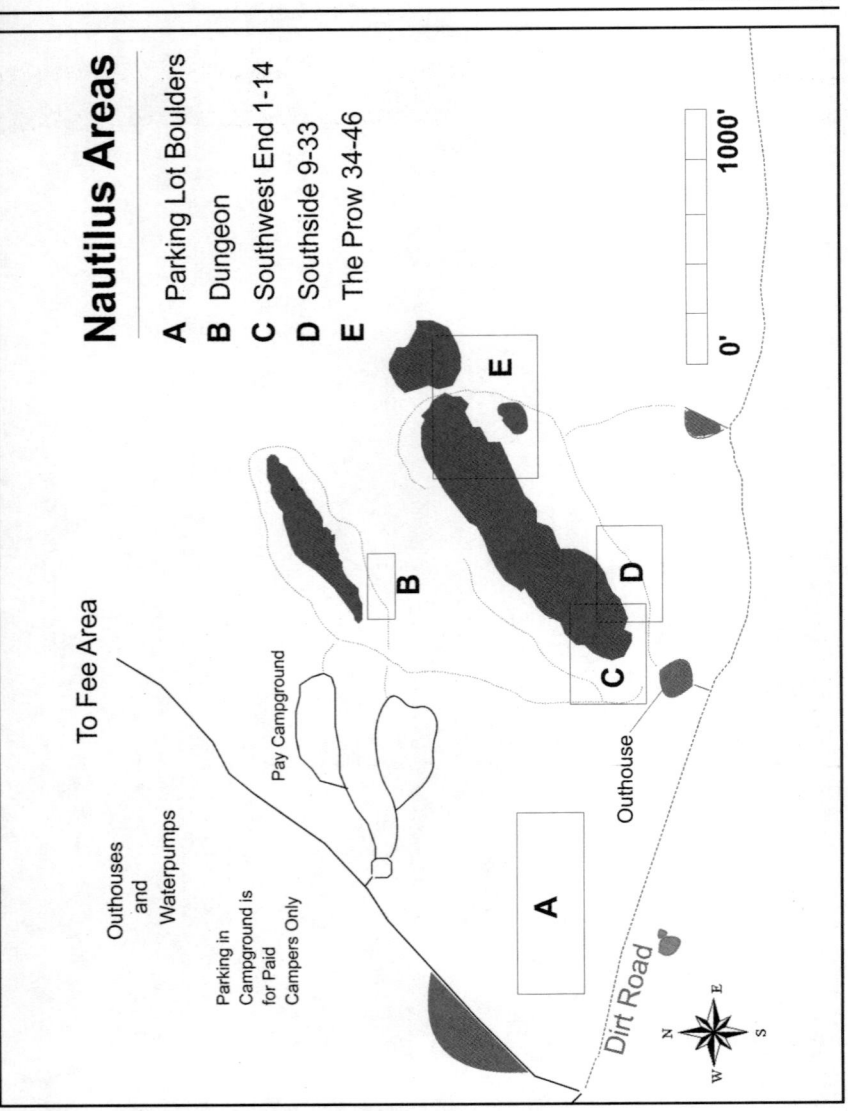

Nautilus Areas

A Parking Lot Boulders
B Dungeon
C Southwest End 1-14
D Southside 9-33
E The Prow 34-46

To Fee Area

Outhouses and Waterpumps

Parking in Campground is for Paid Campers Only

Pay Campground

Outhouse

Dirt Road

0'   1000'

Nautilus

	Area Name	Mileage	Turns*
4	Nautilus	0.2	1st Left

*From exit 329 head East on Vedauwoo Road. Mileage and turns start from where Vedauwoo Road turns to dirt.

Problem Distribution Table

	V0-V3	V4-V7	V8-V10	V11+	Cracks	Total
Quantity	23	12	5	0	24	71

*Total includes projects and unrated problems.

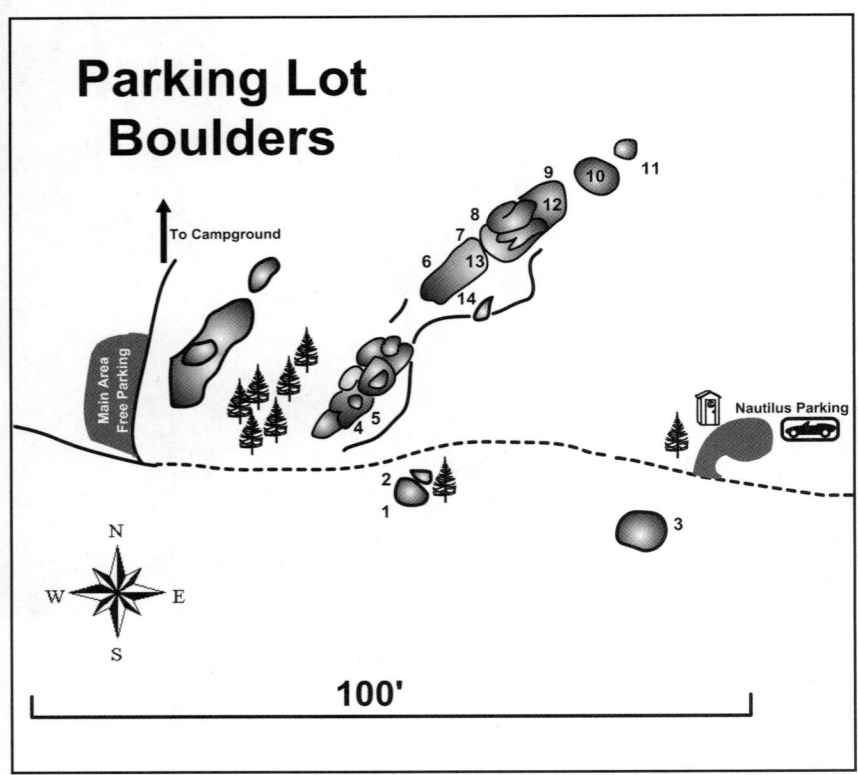

Parking Lot Boulders

1. V0

Climb the left or right side of the hollow flake, on the west facing side of the boulder.

2. V3

Climb the thin seam on the face of the boulder facing the road. There is a little tree growing out of the crack at the top. Grabbing the tree makes the problem much easier.

3. Gill Slab V4

Directly across the road from the parking lot is a large boulder sitting near a fence. Climb the crystally east face.

4. V0-V4

There are several other problems on the fin closest to the road.

5. Road Side Dyno V2

This problem is on the southeast face of the fin closest to the road. Start on good holds down low and right of the obvious flake. Dyno to the lip, just for fun.

6. V1

Sit start using a block with a tree growing out of it.

7. V2

On the right side of the little gap, climb crystals to the top.

8. Sit Down Seam V3

On the northwest side of the short wall just left of a small gap, use the seam for motivation and move straight up on crystals.

9. Bumpcake V1

Boulder the shallow arete that faces the Nautilus and the previous problem, using crystals.

10. Traverse V2

On the next boulder west of the previous is a horizontal seam. Traverse either direction.

11. Traverse V0

Traverse right to left on the short slab, moving up and into a bucket at the lip. This is the first climbable boulder reached from the parking lot when going north.

12. The Red Wave V1

The concave slab just left of the previous problem.

13. 5.8

Sit start the hand crack corner.

14. V0

Lieback flake on the southeast side of the wall.

Parking Lot

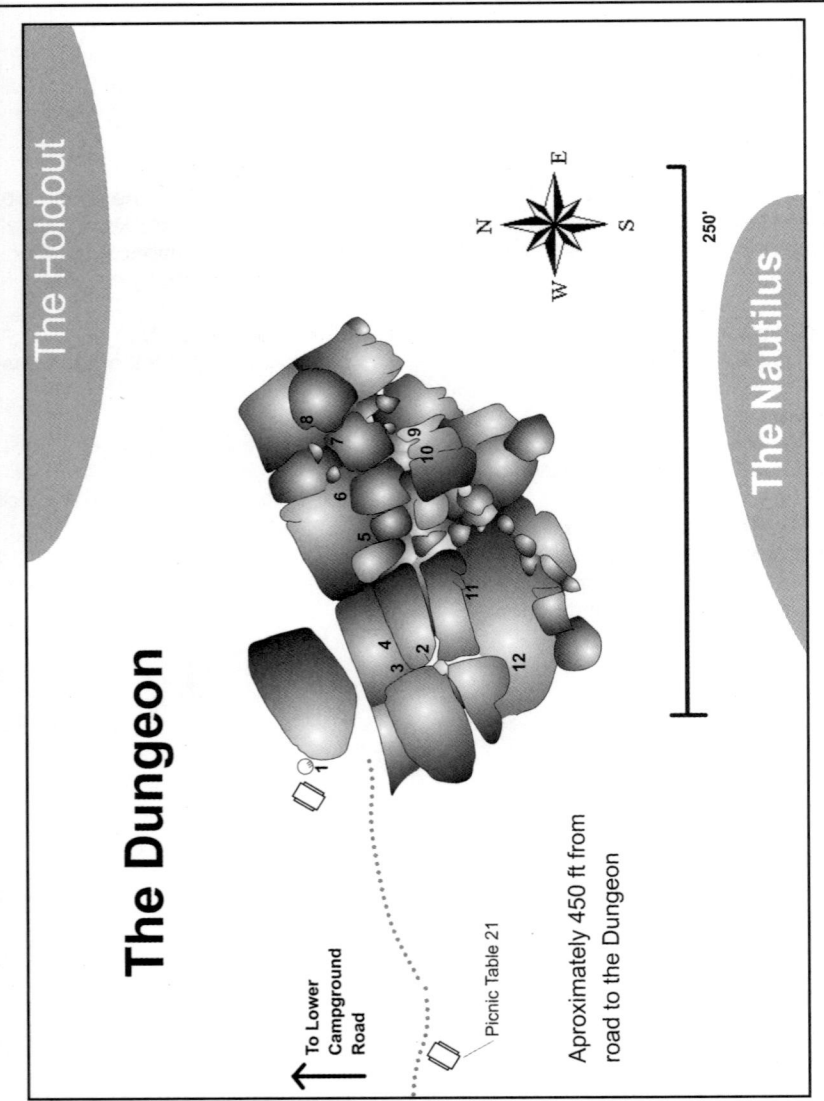

The Dungeon

The Holdout

The Nautilus

250'

To Lower Campground Road

Picnic Table 21

Aproximately 450 ft from road to the Dungeon

1. Enter the Chamber V3

This is located on the prow of the boulder just behind the picnic table. Jump start to slopers, then right hand crystal, throw to top.

2. 5.9

On the shelf, just above the picnic table there is a small A-frame cave. On the back wall, to the left, climb the hand crack.

3. Life Without Parole 5.12

This is the wide crack that splits the small cave. Start on hand jams where the two boulders meet, put your feet above your head and climb up and out of the cave. You shouldn't be hanging upside-down when your done.

4. Project

This problem may have been done. Undercling start, left, to *Life Without Parole*.

5. 5.8

Sit start the hand crack that gets wider as you go up.

6. V5

Really high ball face on good edges. There are bolts on top for a toprope if you're interested in surviving.

7. Lethal Injection V8

This is the really clean face just right of the last A-frame corridor, on the east end of the Dungeon. Using crimps and side pulls, exit left of the seam.

8. Iron Maiden V10

This is the seam/dihedral overhanging problem on the left side of the A-frame. Sit start on hard sloping edges and fire up the seam, finishing on the good hold where the seam terminates. It's a project after that!

In the middle of the Dungeon where the boulders are shortest, go inside the formation and wander to the east end through corridors that give this place it's name. The next two problems are located inside the Dungeon. Both are hard roof cracks.

9. The Warden 5.13

At the far end of the inside of the Dungeon, look for a WIDE crack that closes down. Sit start or "shoulder" start to get established in the uncomfortably wide roof. If you can get in and get your feet above your head, start moving for the good jams and a chance to get your head where it should be.

10. Escape Tunnel 5.12

This is the low roof crack that has a bit of a wide section in it. You get to it before the last problem is reached. Can be done in either direction.

11. 5.9

Hand crack and flake on the south side of the Dungeon's west end.

12. Unknown Problem

Nautilus Boulders

Nautilus: Southwest End

Problems 1-14

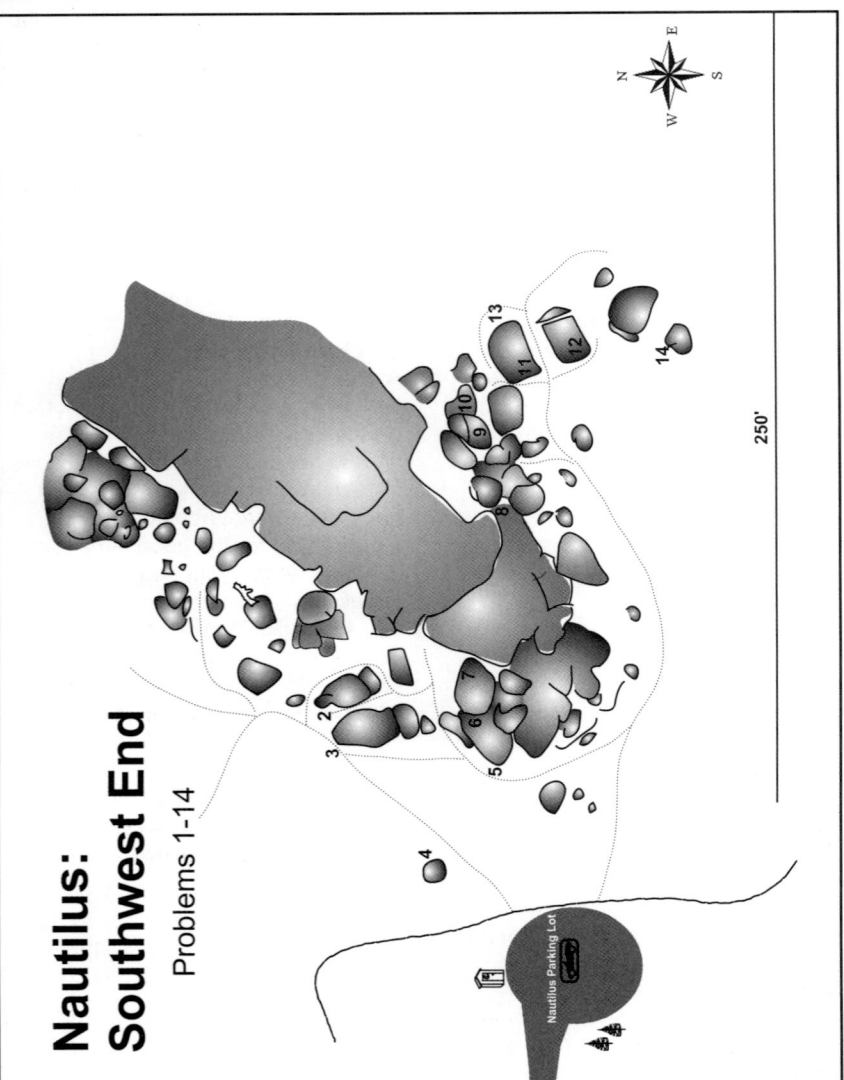

N E S W

250'

Nautilus Parking Lot

The Southwest End Side

1. Sun Up to Sun Down V7

This classic problem is located on the large boulder that is leaning against the middle of the Nautilus (Cool Hand Luke area if you climb routes). Climb up the gently overhanging face on the west side. Start on the good edge facing the formation. Go up on edges and the arete, and undercling the rail up top.

2. The Seal V4

This problem starts on a scoop on the left end of the east most boulder and goes up awkwardly to the top.

Trevor Turmelle on Sun Up Till Sundown. Photo: Davin Bagdonas

Nautilus Boulders

3. Gill Problem V4/5

The large boulder covered with crystals, which touches the trail around the west end of the Nautilus holds this problem. Mantle the crystally face next to the trail, and go up to the better hold and the top.

4. V5

Run, jump, and mantle the side that faces the dungeon.

5. V0-V4

There are several good slabs that come off of the west end of the Nautilus just above the trail. The one in the corridor between the Nautilus and the small boulder with the very eroded trail between, is perhaps the best of them.

6. V3

Above the slabs mentioned in the previous description is a boulder, sitting on a shelf, with a scoop on it's face. The scoop is V3 and can be sit started.

7. V6

The back of the boulder mentioned in the previous description is V6 crimp pulling up a vertical face.

The Nautilus South Side

Problems on the south side of the Nautilus are described from west to east along the mingling trails in the boulders, or from left to right when looking at the Nautilus from Vedauwoo road.

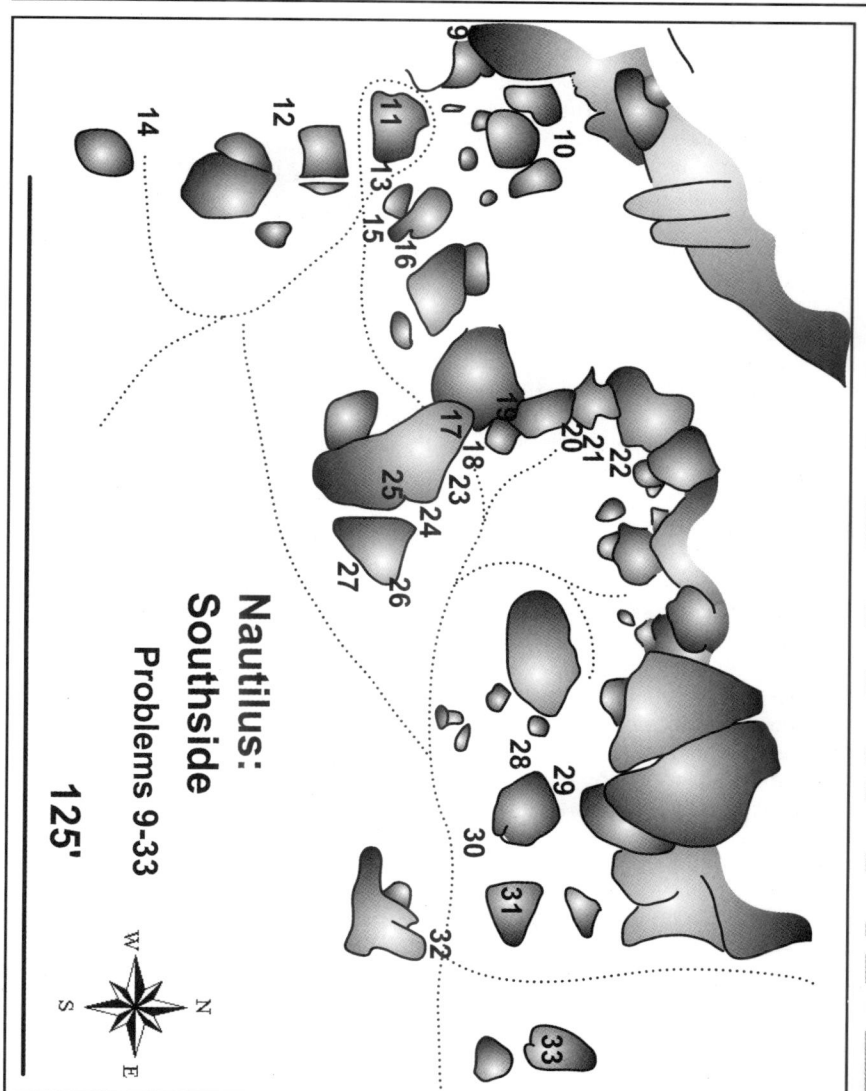

Nautilus Boulders

Nautilus:
Southside

Problems 9-33

125'

8. Help V9

Walk uphill and left from the previous problem. Go through a corridor of boulders on the left and The Nautilus on the right. Climb down into the hole at the end of the corridor. Help is on the left wall as you go down. Sit start on edges and use the arete to go up and finish left after a lengthy traverse escape.

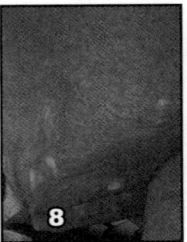

9. Lucky You 5.12

Go left, walking in front of the prow mentioned in the previous description and follow the faint trail. This problem is located in an elevated cave under where two boulders touch on the left side of the trail. Sit start the off width roof on good hand jams and continue until you have the last jam in the top of the roof where the crack shuts down.

10. The Tempest V10

Follow directions to the previous problem, but go right and up onto a boulder to go through a cave where this problem is located. Start on the left end of a horizontal seam, at the back of a small roof. Go right along the seam, around the corner, and up to the apex of the boulder.

11. V6

Pull on crystals just right of the rounded corner on the prow of the boulder.

12 . Project

Just before the large boulder that holds the previous problem, go right around a perfect triangle face to the slabby south side of the boulder.

Climb the steep left end on crimps and less. This problem may have been done, but is now missing the holds it once had.

13. The Nest V9?

Using blocky holds midway up the boulder's east face, pull into the crystally, less-than-vertical upper face .

14. A Little Crack, A little Face, It looks Like An Interesting Evening. 5.11-

Climb out the back of a small roof using the flared crack. Then move up the face on crystals and edges.

15. 5.7

Sit start the dihedral crack.

16. 5.8

Climb the crack in the back of the huge flake.

17. 5.10+

There are two problems here. Both start on a large jug and go up on flared jams around where the large upper boulder sits on the lower wall. Go out either side.

18. 5.9

Sit start the short hand crack on the right end of the corridor where the trail goes under the roof. Another start is on the flake to the left of the crack.

19. V5

Pull on crisp edges on the lip of the boulder to gain some juice for the

Following pages: Steve Millard on Soke 'em Inside Her. Photo: Ken Driese

crystally mantle.

20. Banana Hammock 5.11+
Start in the back of a flared roof crack
and jam out to the lip.

21. 5.8 to 5.10
There are four problems that jam out
the sides of the wedged block uphill
from the previous problem.

22. 5.9
Climb the perfect hand crack dihedral
set above smaller boulders that make
for an optional sit start.

23. Project
Small crimps up the just past vertical
face. Goes to the obvious crystals up
higher.

24. Soak 'em Inside Her V5
Sit start, lieback seam to crystal pulls
at the lip of the boulder. This problem
was "the" problem at The Nautilus
through the late 90s.

25. 5.10
This is the hand to thin hand sized
crack located in the hallway between
boulders, left of the previous problem.
The feet are a little crumbly.

26. Mantle V2/3
Mantle the jug onto the less-than-vertical face. Easier if you are shorter since
your butt will fit the balance point.

27. V0
Follow the positive holds.

28. 5.11
This is the flared crack problem that
begins under a small roof and has
crumbly feet. Negotiate the flared jams
to gain better up top.

29. Project V5
Stand start on rails then top out on

crystals. Sit start on steep face below for project.

30. Impossible Flake? Project
This problem has never been done although everybody has tried it.

31. V0
The west-facing slab. Try it without hands for a warm-up.

32. V1
This is the short slab problem on the south side of the trail with a small bulb of rock used for the start.

33. V3
Super problem for its grade. Where the trail goes up slabs toward the middle of the Nautilus, go right into the aspen grove. Climb the flared seam to face moves up top.

34. Ant Crack 5.10-
Though 5.10, it gets a little high. Where the aspen grove meets the Nautilus in the middle, this crack goes from right to left above a small slab. It's located on the portion of the Nautilus that is farthest south.

35. 5.10+
Above the aspen grove and the previous problem. Prominent horizontal crack that is traversed from right to left. Don't fall off the crux!

36. Wade's Face V2
On the top of the Nautilus is a sloping ramp with large boulders. The boulders on the highest end hold this problem. High ball the perfect crimps up the clean face on the east side of the large boulder.

37. Derin's Problem V2/3
Almost on top of the Nautilus on the south side, east end is a large sunken ledge

Nautilus Boulders

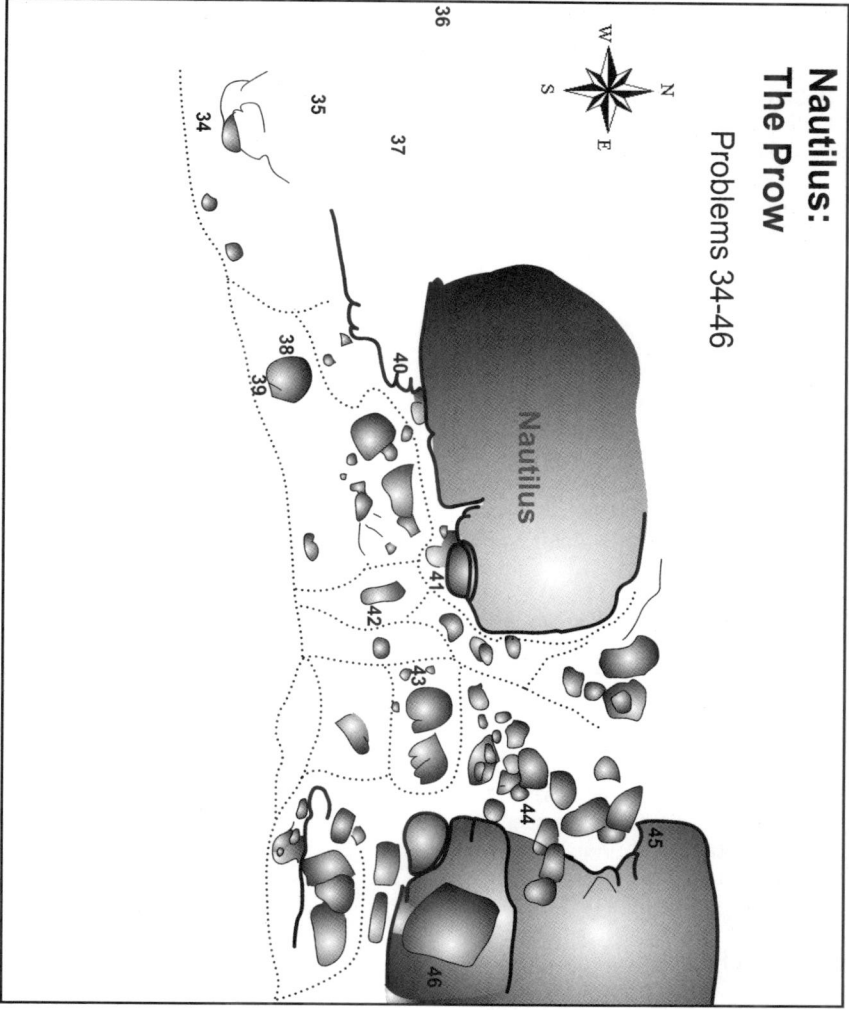

**Nautilus:
The Prow**

Problems 34-46

**Opposite: Bevan Frost on Cupcake, 5.10c.
Photo: Joe Johnson.**

with a grassy landing. At the end of the ledge is a featured boulder. Climb it and enjoy the view.

38 Gill Problem V3
Climb the tall slab.

39. Cup Cake 5.10
The most famous high ball in Vedauwoo, and rightly so. Clean jams up the right-leaning hand crack that sits next to the trail. Down climb the tree.

40. 5.11
From the previous problem, follow the trail up switchbacks and past a large boulder sitting out right. Just past this, on the left wall of the corridor formed by the Nautilus on the left and boulders on the right, is a small roof with a crack in it. Climb down and out of the cave and finish on the wide crack, turn the lip.

41. Various Cracks 5.10-5.11
Various warm up cracks on south side of the middle parallel space pillar. Exit right.

42. Gill Face V4/5
There is a large independent boulder on the hillside below the previous problem, or below the Nautilus' east end. John Gill climbed variations on the face using the abundant crystals.

43. Traverse V1
Just south and downhill from the very east end of the Nautilus is a short wall with a horizontal crack. Go left to right or finish somewhere in between by going up. A good warm-up if you're doing routes.

44. 5.11
In the corridor between the formations there is a large chock stone. Under it is this problem, which is a finger crack.

45. 5.12
To get to this problem, go up to the saddle between the Nautilus and the tower to the east. Then go down into the corridor between the two and walk north (toward the dark side). On the right wall is a very thin, less-than-fingers crack in a dihedral. Go right at the horizontal and down climb.

46. Balanced Boulder Project
On the very top of the formation that sits just east of the Nautilus proper, is a large cube of a stone. The east side is a beautiful overhanging face that will surely become super classic!

Nautilus Boulders

Central

Opposite: Nathan Manley on Problem 4 in Box Canyon.
Photo: Davin Bagdonas.

63

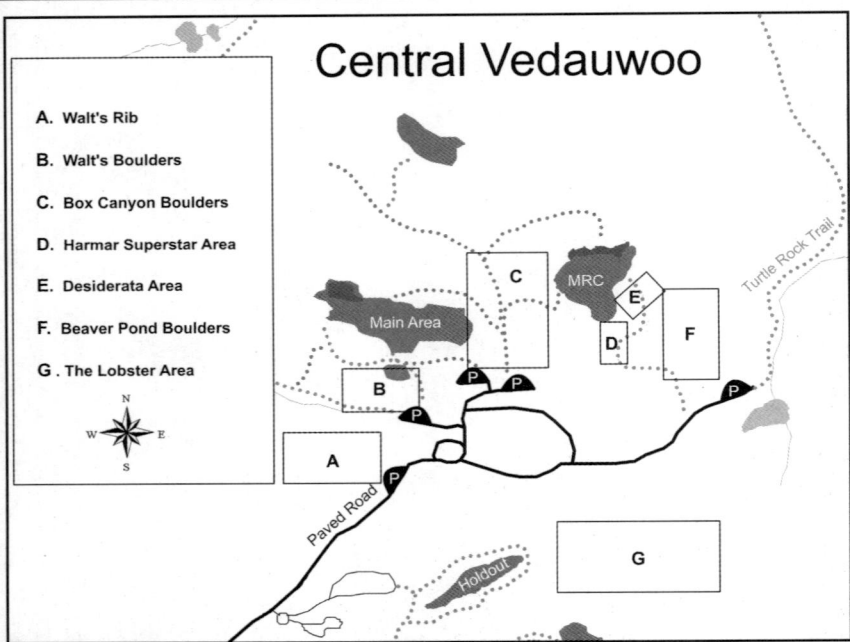

Central Vedauwoo

A. Walt's Rib

B. Walt's Boulders

C. Box Canyon Boulders

D. Harmar Superstar Area

E. Desiderata Area

F. Beaver Pond Boulders

G. The Lobster Area

Directions

From Interstate 80, off the Vedauwoo exit, follow the Vedauwoo road to where the pavement ends. Go left following the pavement or park in the paved parking lot or in the dirt along the fence just before the pavement goes left. It costs to park in central Vedauwoo, so parking up above might be the answer. However, if you don't mind paying the fee or have a pass, follow the paved road.

Your first left will bring you to the parking for Walt's Rib and Walt's Boulders. To reach Box Canyon Boulders, follow paved roads to the lowest parking lot. To reach the Beaver Ponds, Har Mar Superstar, Desiderata, and the Lobster areas, go right at the first right turn on the paved road and follow it to it's end.

Central

	Area Name	Mileage	Turns*
3	Central	NA	2nd Left

*From exit 329 head East on Vedauwoo Road. Mileage and turns start from the second cattle guard.

Problem Distribution Table

	V0-V3	V4-V7	V8-V10	V11+	Cracks	Total
Quantity	16	18	9	3	16	117

*Total includes projects and unrated problems.

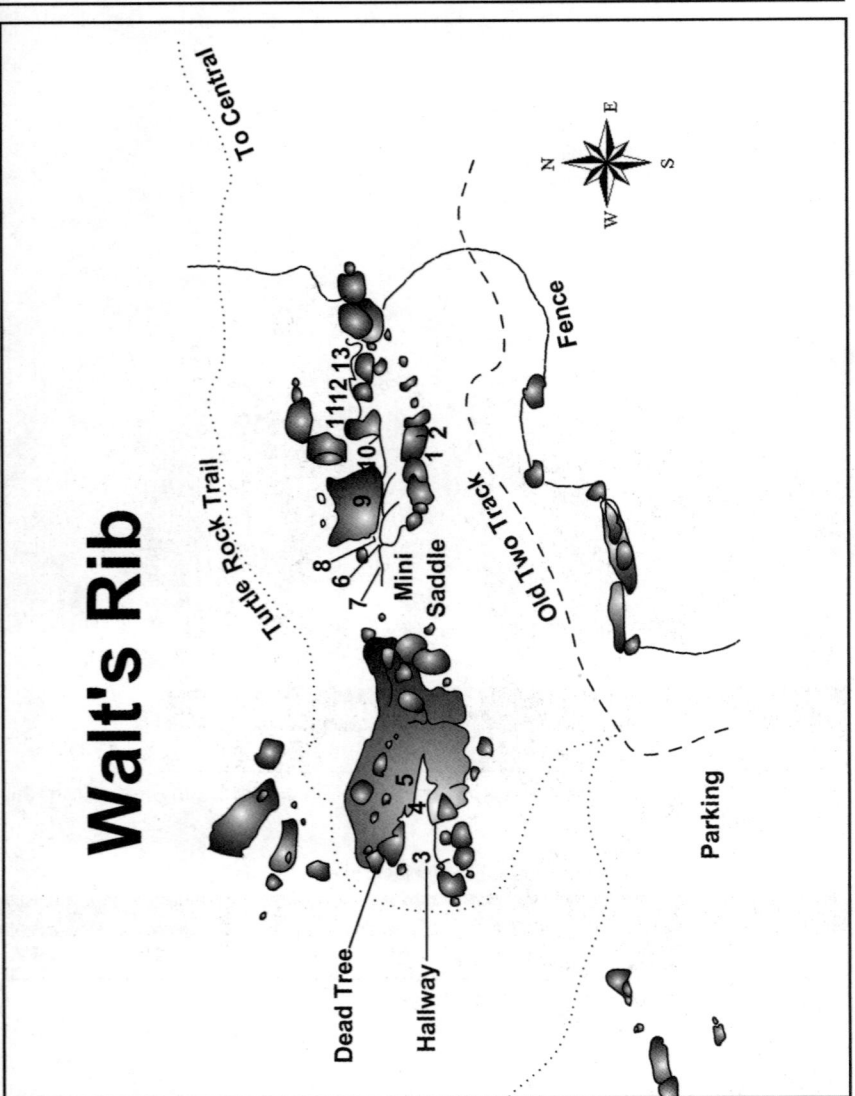

Central Vedauwoo

Walt's Rib

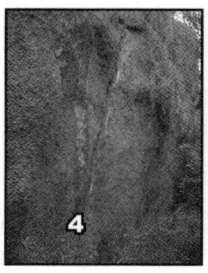
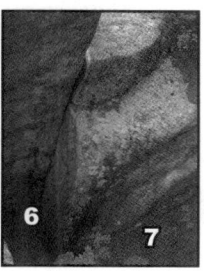
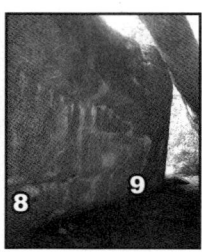

Walt's Rib

1. V5
Start on the side pulls at the base of the tall slab. Go up the slab

2. V5
Follow the thin seam up the tall slab.

3. 5.10a
Sit start the flared crack across from the burned tree stump.

4. 5.10c
This is the splitter right leaning finger crack in the hallway. Sit start it.

5. V0-V2
There are various slab problems on the north wall of the hallway.

6. Out of Site 5.11b
The super splitter hand crack. Really good!

7. V5
Start on the jug and go to slopers. This problem is on the wall just right of the previous problem.

8. V1
Lieback the flake on the east side of the big flat boulder.

9. V5/6
Sit start on slopers before moving a bit right on crimps in the little cave.

10. N.F.L. Dyno Project V10?
Dyno from the sloper rail to the lip of the big flat boulder. Could be started lower along the base of the rail.

Central Vedauwoo

11. The Swan V9?
Vedauwoo's hardest slab problem? This is the tall dish/slab with not much on it.
12. 5.8
Climb the hand crack.
13. 5.10c
Sit start hand to tips crack. Splitter but short.

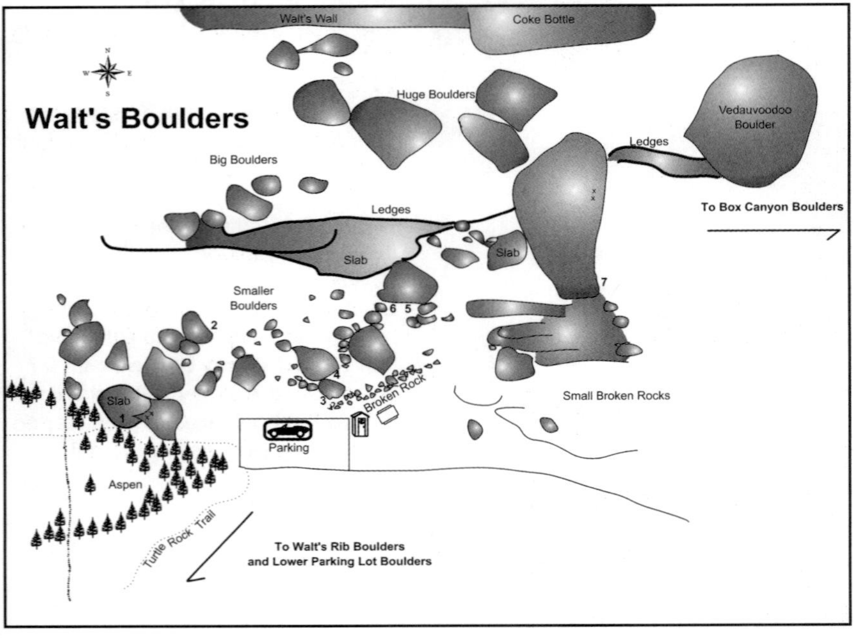

Walt's Boulders

Walt's Wall

Coke Bottle

Huge Boulders

Vedauvoodoo Boulder

Big Boulders

Ledges

Ledges

To Box Canyon Boulders

Slab

Slab

Smaller Boulders

6 5

2

7

4

3

Broken Rock

Small Broken Rocks

Slab

1

Parking

Aspen

Turtle Rock Trail

To Walt's Rib Boulders
and Lower Parking Lot Boulders

Central Vedauwoo

Walt's Boulders

1. V6
A tall arete over a gentle slab. From the parking lot, take the Turtle Rock Trail west to the nearest boulder. On toprope it's 5.12+. A proud send for the brave boulderer.

2. Burning Bush V8
From a sit start on the lowest part of the rail in the roof, on a triangular hold, move left and up to the lip of the roof. Pull onto the lip and onto the slab toward the featured turtle shell texture. If you're wearing shorts and the stinging nettles are growing, you'll feel the burning bush.

Mydland's Solo Tension Boulder

3. The Gill Seam V6
Climb the thin seam with a rivet in it. Watch the landing, or climb it like Gill did-with a diaper on his head. This was an aid boulder problem in the early 1960s that went free on John Gill's arrival to Vedauwoo in 1967.

4. V2
Crisp edges on the back of the Mydland Boulder.

Central Vedauwoo

Central Vedauwoo

5. The Dyno V8
The really good and tall vertical face on cobbles that starts on the low, good cobble. The V8 part is way up there.
6. V2
The featured left side of the boulder.
7. Gill Problem V7?
Start on the low end of the huge boulder on a flat undercling. There are zero feet as you reach for the lip.

Box Canyon Boulders

1. The Piana Mantle V8?
Between the west side Veda-Voodoo Boulder and the picnic table on the elevated shelf, is a long hollow cave. On the east end, mantle cobbles up a shallow dish. Paul Piana left this as a project, but it has since been done.

2. Ankle Breaker V1-V2
This is the distinctive slab, facing southwest in an open flat area above the gazebo. Go straight up the southwest facing slab, above the badly placed flake. There are several variations most likely contrived to avoid the flake.

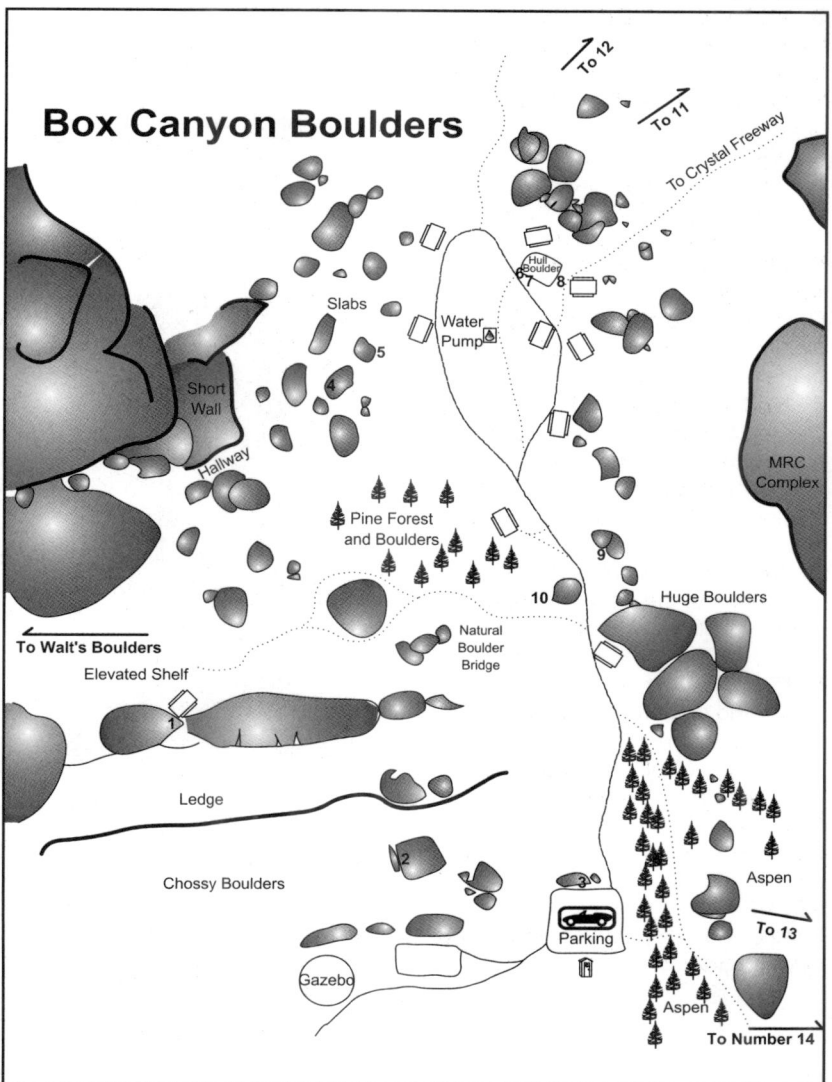

Box Canyon Boulders

To 12

To 11

To Crystal Freeway

Hull Boulder

Slabs

Water Pump

Short Wall

Hallway

MRC Complex

Pine Forest and Boulders

To Walt's Boulders

Elevated Shelf

Huge Boulders

Natural Boulder Bridge

Ledge

Chossy Boulders

Aspen

To 13

Parking

Gazebo

Aspen

To Number 14

Central Vedauwoo

3. Parking Lot Off Width 5.11b
On the north side of the parking lot there is a very short and crumbly off width. Sit start it with your feet uphill and up.

4. V4
Start low on the right side of the face on a good edge. Follow the face left to the apex of the boulder.

5. Three and a Half Foot Assassin V9
Grab the crimp above your head. One move wonder yourself to the lip of the rock.

6. Hull's Boulder V0
The left side of the slab along the prow. One of the oldest problems in the country. Done prior to 1966 (rumored to have been done in the late 1950s).

7. John Horn's Direct V0
The center of the slab. Also done prior to 1966, but later than the previous.

8. Fire Walker V3
Follow the diagonaling scoop and bulge above the scoop along the south side of Hull's Boulder. There used to be a fire pit under it.

9. 5.11b
Sit start the short finger crack roof, then turn the lip.

10. V2
The prow of the boulder opposite the paved road/trail.

11. Get Yourself a College Girl V7

This problem faces south and is uphill and across the saddle from the Crystal Freeway. It's just below the boulder that looks like a ground squirrel. Follow the long, gently rising finger crack from right to left and finish where the crack shuts down.

12. 5.8

Climb the hand crack.

To find the next two problems its best to get a local to show you the way.

13. Cincinnati Sui-Slide 5.12a

This problem is on the slabs to the south of the gully. About half way up the blocky slabs that face west, is a hidden cave (smokers cave) that holds this roof crack. Start downhill and jam along the crack, turn with the crack up the sui-slide and exit on wide crack moves at the exit of the cave.

14. The Biggest Tits in Country Music 5.11c

Climb out the roof crack where two cracks come together. There are jugs at the lip to assist you.

Central Vedauwoo

**Bob Stuckert on Biggest Tits in Country Music.
Photo: Bob Stuckert Collection.**

The Beaver Pond Boulders

1. V6
Start on a crescent, on slimpers. Pull to the crack/seam and follow it as it leans left. Going right, dyno wise is a project.

The next boulder is located just left of the gate as you are walking down Turtle Rock Trail.

2. The Borg V11
Start on the far left side of the right leaning, diagonaling seam. Use slopers to move right to a mini cobble/inclusion and a crystally sloper. Straight up on nothing gets you to the lip.

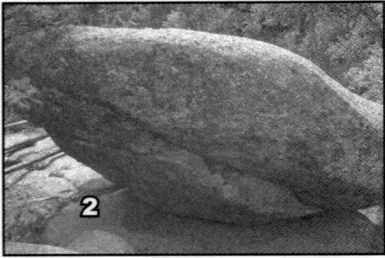

3. V4
Sit start the left end/arete of the undercut slab on a good horizontal. Follow the arete and right face.

4. V3
Sit start the middle of the undercut, featured slab on a crisp edge. Take good features up the slab to the top.

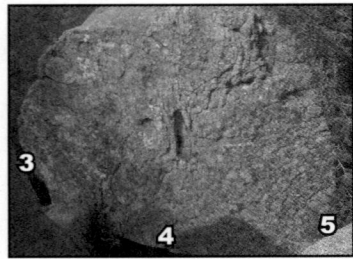

5. V6
The right side of the featured slab. Sit start and follow the prow.

6. Project
Sit start the low cobble.

7. Bob 69 Project
Just before the stream on a steep overhanging face. "Bob 69" is spray-painted at the start. Traverse right along a horizontal, then move up and right to a slopey top out.

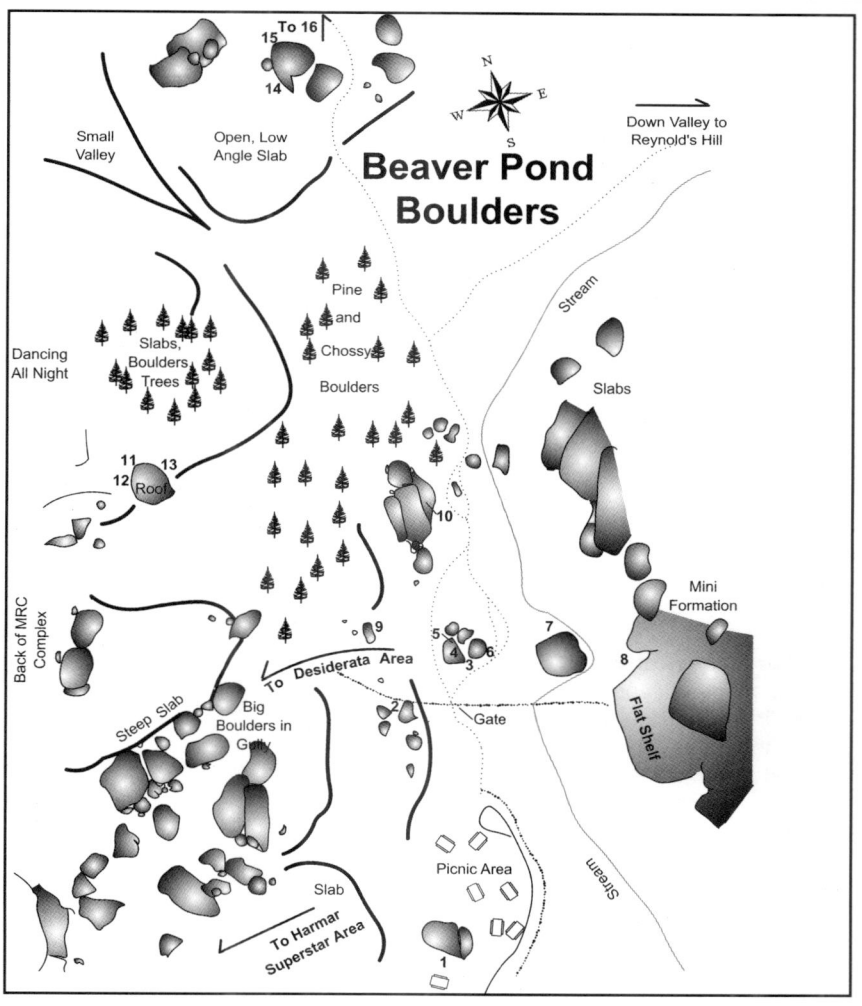

To 16

15

14

Small
Valley

Open, Low
Angle Slab

N
W — E
S

Down Valley to
Reynold's Hill

Beaver Pond
Boulders

Dancing
All Night

Pine
and
Chossy
Boulders

Slabs,
Boulders,
Trees

Stream

Slabs

11   13
12   Roof

10

Back of MRC
Complex

Mini
Formation

9

5

7

4

6

8

To Desiderata Area

3

Steep Slab

Big
Boulders in
Gully

2

Gate

Flat Shelf

Slab

To Harmar
Superstar Area

Picnic Area

Stream

1

Central Vedauwoo

Central Vedauwoo

8. V2

The featured prow above the shelf of rock. There's a sloper up there.

9. V3

Sit start the big cobble and yank up the vertical face to choss.

10. Old Yeller V5

This is a super slab! A bad left foot and a poor right crimp get you started. Aim for the cobbles up the dish.

11. Best in Show V5/6

Start in the back of the cave on the right side of a big flake/rail. Follow it left, transition to another flake/rail and take it to the lip. Then the crux.

12. Good Vibrations V7

The start is the same as the previous. Move right/straight through the cave on smaller flakes. Turn the lip and climb into the previous problem's exit.

13. V5

The tall slab with a hole in the rock under it.

14. Bombay Hooker V5/7

Jump start into an above head undercling, then move around the left side of the "nose" and shoot for the death star dish sloper and top out. Final move is extremely height dependent.

15. V8

Start low on a slopey horizontal on boulder's right side. Continue up on good edges to the top.

16. The Red Snapper V13

Vedauwoo's hardest so far! To get to it, continue walking the Turtle Rock Trail past The Bombay Hooker Boulder, along the open hill side/slabs. Just past 2 cut dead trees on the right of the trail,

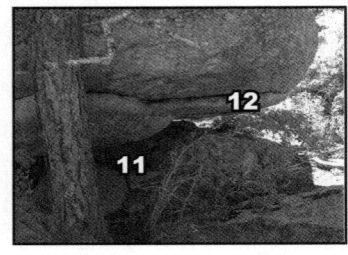

move right and walk downhill through boulders. Then back left to a small cove of boulders, Red Snapper is the right leaning crack.

**Below: Andy Raether on Bombay Hooker.
Photo: Josh Helke.**

Desiderata

Har Mar Superstar

**Opposite: Andy Raether on Har Mar Superstar.
Photo: Josh Helke.**

Har Mar Superstar Area
To get to Har Mar Superstar, park by the outhouse next to Turtle Rock Trail's East trailhead. The picture above was taken from here.

1. Enter the Realm V8
Move right along the sloping lip for 10 feet, until it turns the arete, then go up the slab.

2. Har Mar Superstar V12
Start on the lowest crystally sloper rail in the cave to the right of the dead leaning tree. Move out the roof on a flake and some edges. Not much at the lip, but you have to use it if you want to mantle onto the slab.

3. Project
The short roof crack with edges in it.

Central Vedauwoo

4. V0
The arete.
5. V2
Climb the right leaning seam.
6. Gamlin V8
Start on the big jug then traverse right on slopers throw to lip. You can also go straight up at V0 or jump start the finish at V3.
7. 5.10b
This problem is located uphill from the Har Mar Superstar area at the base of the formation. It is the gently overhanging hand crack that faces south.
8. Unknown Crack Dihedral
Looks like 5.10 or so but maybe hasn't been done?
9. Yellow Wall V8
Start low left hand crimp and high right hand crimp then slap up to belly on left side of wall. Exit left. Pulling the final bulge is a project that has not yet gone.

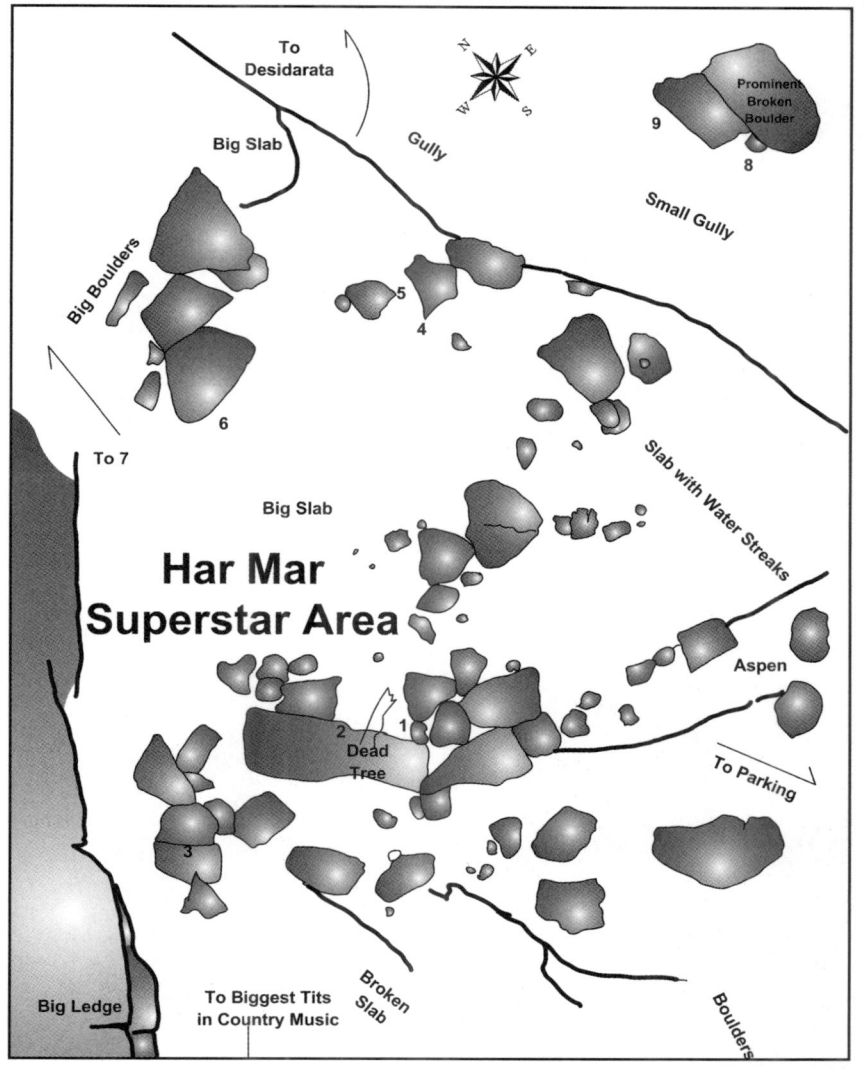

To Desidarata

Gully

N E
W S

Prominent Broken Boulder

9

8

Big Slab

Small Gully

Big Boulders

5

4

6

To 7

Slab with Water Streaks

Big Slab

Har Mar Superstar Area

Aspen

2 1

Dead Tree

To Parking

3

Big Ledge

To Biggest Tits in Country Music

Broken Slab

Boulders

Central Vedauwoo

Desiderata Area

1. Desiderata
5.12d
A perfect splitter, fifteen foot, off width, roof. Starts very wide and narrows to stacks at the lip, then shuts down completely after the lip. Start inverted at the far end and crank all the way out the spectacular roof.

2. Tyco Shop
5.12b/c
Start low in the good hand jams under the fifteen foot roof. Move out on tight hands and negotiate off fingers at the lip.

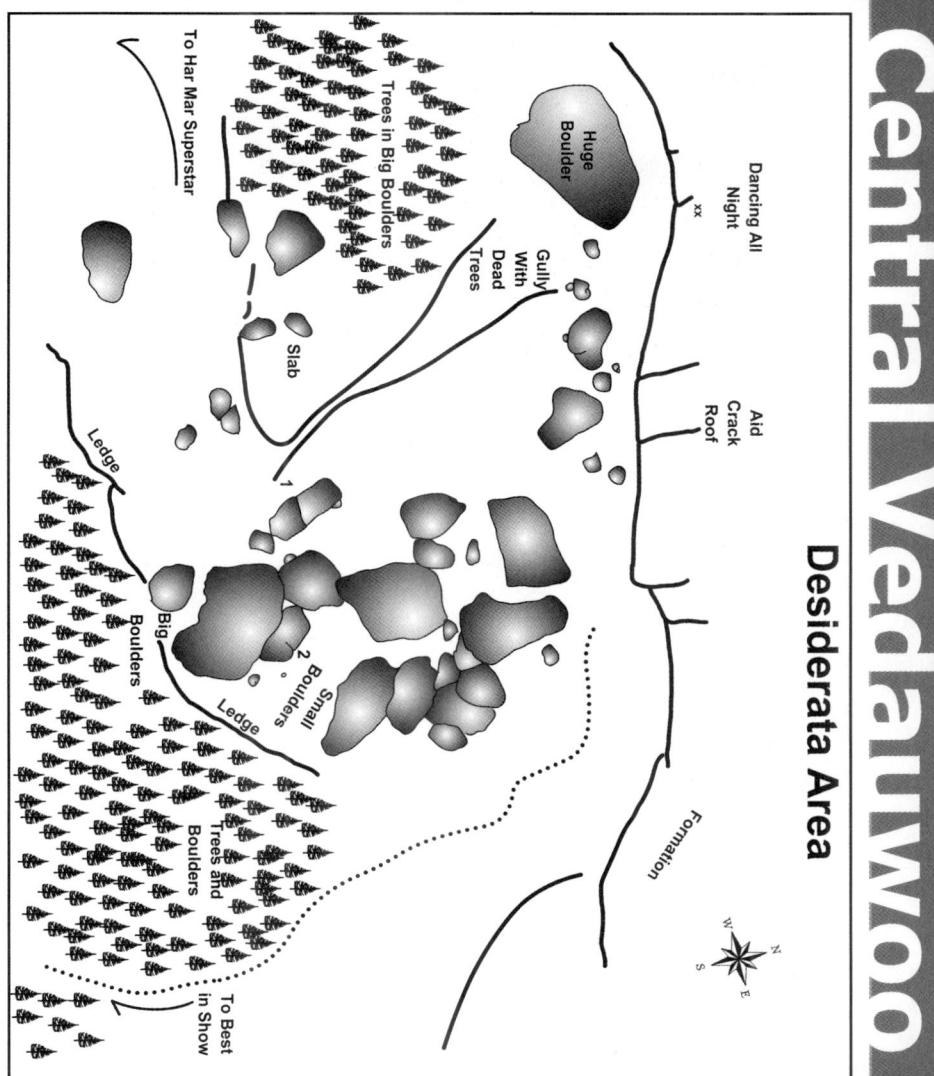

Central Vedauwoo

Desiderata Area

To Har Mar Superstar

Trees in Big Boulders

Huge Boulder

Dancing All Night

xx

Gully With Dead Trees

Aid Crack Roof

Slab

Ledge

Big Boulders

Ledge

2 Boulders

Small

Formation

Trees and Boulders

To Best in Show

N
W E
S

FOR MORE INFO ON VEDAUWOO BOULDERING, BE SURE TO CHECK OUT VOOBOULDERING.COM

Justin Edl on Tyco Shop.
Photo: Davin Bagdonas.

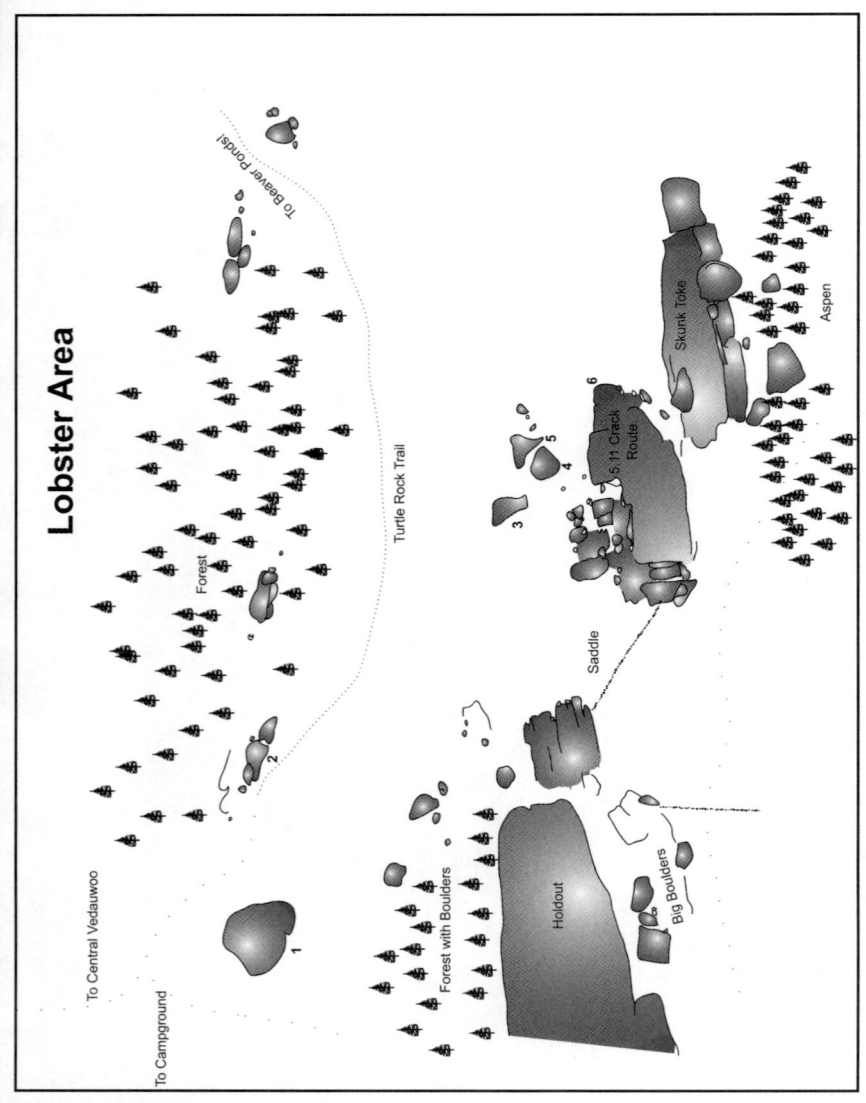

Central Vedauwoo

Lobster Area

To Central Vedauwoo

To Campground

Forest with Boulders

Holdout

Big Boulders

Saddle

1

2

3

4

5

6

5.11 Crack Route

Skunk Toke

Aspen

Forest

Turtle Rock Trail

To Beaver Ponds!

The Lobster Area

1. 5.11a
The very tall dihedral crack on the huge boulder in the woods. Should or could be a short route.

2. V2
This is right along the Turtle Rock Trail. Grab the sloping edge and mantle for a reach at the lip.

3. Warm Up Block V0-V3
Various problems can be done on the angular block.

4. The Lobster V5
Sit start the lowest sloping rail under the arete. Pull out the gentle overhang to a pinch on the arete and use another pinch to gain the lobster move. Go up the arete. The original version stayed on the left side of the arete and was rated V7. Both are good problems.

5. Clam Opener V8
Sit start the short arete on pinches. Go for the good edge out left and up.

6. Project
The prow of the short formations east end. From a side pull and undercling.

Central Vedauwoo

Nat's

Dave Nash on Nat's Three Star Roof
Photo: Matt Williams.

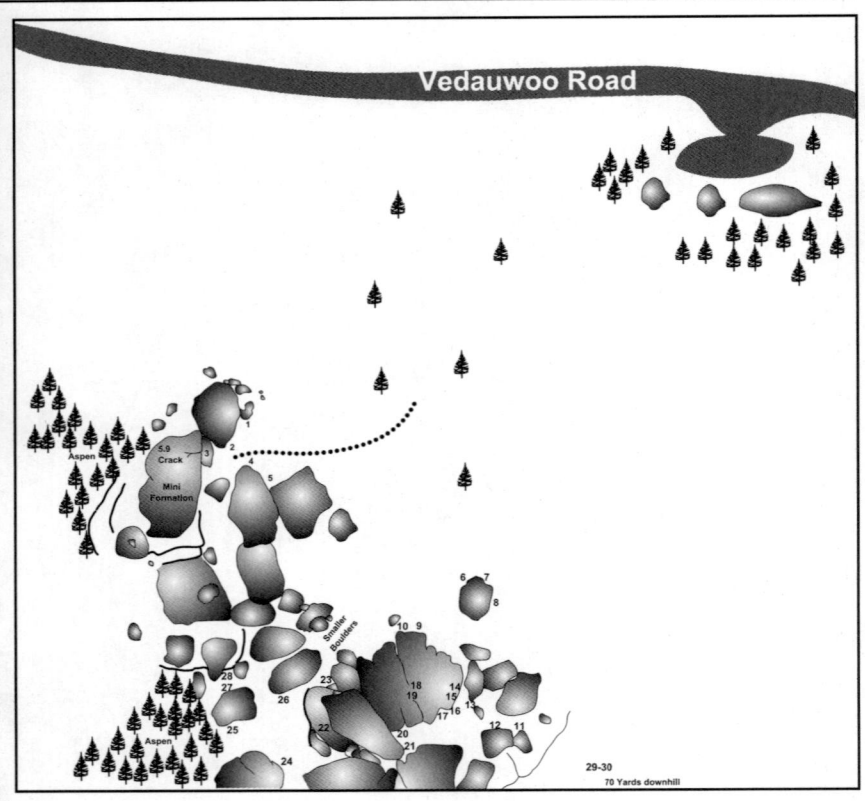

Vedauwoo Road

Nat's

	Area Name	Mileage	Turns*
5	Nat's	0.6	1st Right

*From exit 329 head East on Vedauwoo Road. Mileage and turns start from where Vedauwoo Road turns to dirt.

Directions

To get to this bouldering area abounding in good crack problems, go down the Vedauwoo Road, beyond where it turns to gravel, and beyond the Nautilus parking area (700T). Park at a small turnout on the right (south) side of the road just before road 700H.

Problem Distribution Table

	V0-V3	V4-V7	V8-V10	V11+	Cracks	Total
Quantity	14	3	1	0	10	30

*Total includes projects and unrated problems.

1. Green Tambourine V1
Step off the large block on good holds.

2. Green Room V4
This is the big green slab next to the tall hand crack. Start on obvious big crystals to surmount the undercut foot of the slab. Path of least resistance leads to the top of this highball.

3. 5.9
Really tall. Bones may be encountered. Basically a solo. Needs cleaning.

4. Arete V0+
Excellent arete climbing. Some jack ass bolted this but the bolts are gone. Site of famed Vedauwoo Bolt Relocation Program. Bonanza!

5. 5.7
The hand to off width dihedral crack.

6. Knee Popper V3
Starting from the same hold as the previous problem. Go up and left to top out.

7. Shin Popper V4
Start on a blocky hold and traverse left around the bulge. Then up on slopers.

8. Project
Less than vertical face on crimps and poor seam thing.

9. 5.10-
Climb the flared thin crack above the small boulder that could ruin your landing from this problem that's located to the left of the big crack.

10. 5.9
Climb the short flared hand crack that is right of the big crack (back of

Nat's 3 Star

Nat's Three Star Roof).

11. Bloody Hug V3
Sit start on the prow of this boulder using a bad edge out left and a better hold out right. Slap up the prow.

12. Around the World V2
Traverse right to left along the lip of the boulder that gently overhangs around its girth. Mantle on the opposite side from where you started.

13. V3
Crystals up the tall boulder.

14. 5.9+
Jam the thin (finger) crack all the way up. Beware of resident bats in the depths of this good problem.

15. 5.7
Use face and crack moves to climb right into the finger crack of the previous problem.

16. Texas Wiener V3
Sit start on a jug and motivate into the thinner climbing above.

17. V3
Sit start the crack.

18. Levitation 69 V7
Crank through Nat's Three Star Roof then go right along the flake in the roof. Raw body tension is needed to gain the start of problem 9, then continue traversing right on good holds to finish on problem 8.

19. Nat's 3 Star Roof 5.11a
Very good crack problem! Start as far back as possible in the long roof on good jams. Crank all the way out to the lip and mantle on insecure jams. Top out, go left till you can get down, or jump off.

20. Classic V3
Follow the right leaning seam up the just past vertical wall until it runs out and you can use the crimp flakes to top out. The sit start is harder. Really good problem!

21. 5.11+
This is the roof/corner that ends with a mantle on a crystal covered face. Really awkward.

22. Spinning the Wind 5.12-
Under where the two boulders meet, start in hand jams. Move into fist jams and continue through the wide crack. Don't get your knee stuck!

23. 5.11+
Finger crack dihedral. Wish it were longer.

24. V8?
Start on the low white stained flake. Move right on poor crimps, then go straight up on the crystally edge.

25. V0
The right leaning rail that is mantled to gain the top.
26. Slopey Rail V0
The right leaning rail.
27. V2
Follow thin, left leaning seams to the lip of the boulder.
28. Vertical Violation 5.10
Follow the zig zag flake past a mantle.
29. IHOP V3
Work your way up stacked seams and underclings.
30. V3
Thin broken cracks to the top.
31. The Crap Artist V 5.13a
This is the overhanging finger crack at the base of the formation, hidden in a corridor. From the parking lot look up at the formation to locate the hand crack in a small dihedral, above a slab. The base of the crack, which is hidden from view, is the problem. Sit starting the thing is a project!

Nat's 3 Star

Vedauwoo Roadless Area, Medicine Bow National Forest Erik Molvar photo

Join Biodiversity Conservation Alliance to help protect Vedauwoo and other spectacular roadless recreation areas in the Medicine Bow National Forest. When you make your tax-deductible donation to BCA, you're supporting a staff of full-time professionals dedicated to protecting wildlife and special places and ensuring that when industrial developments do occur on public lands, they are as sustainable as possible. As a member of BCA, you'll also receive alerts when logging or drilling projects threaten important public lands, get the inside scoop on the latest conservation issues, and receive info on free guided hikes to wild places at risk. To join, simply photocopy and fill out the form below:

Name_____

Address_____

Email_____

$100	Sponsor
$200 and up	Patron
$35	Basic annual membership
$20	Student/low income

Mail your check to:
Biodiversity Conservation Alliance, P.O. Box 1512, Laramie, WY 82070

Dirty Deeds

	Area Name	Mileage	Turns*	Page
6	Dirty Deeds	1.3	6th Left	96

*From exit 329 head East on Vedauwoo Road. Mileage and turns start from where Vedauwoo Road turns to dirt.

Directions

Off of Vedauwoo Road to the left (north), after 700E is passed on the right, you will see road 700I. Pull in, park and walk north to the first boulders, closest to the parking area. On the north facing wall, with fire pits below it, just beyond the parking, look for two tall crack problems. A wide crack on the right side of the wall and a fist to a bit wider crack on the left of the wall are the first problems you come to when walking north. The rest of the boulders are located throughout the area, down the hill. The largest part of the big boulders at the bottom of the hill forms an a-frame cave. On the right wall of this cave is the crack problem Dirty Deeds.

Problem Distribution Table

	V0-V3	V4-V7	V8-V10	V11+	Cracks	Total
Quantity	0	1	0	0	5	6

*Total includes projects and unrated problems.

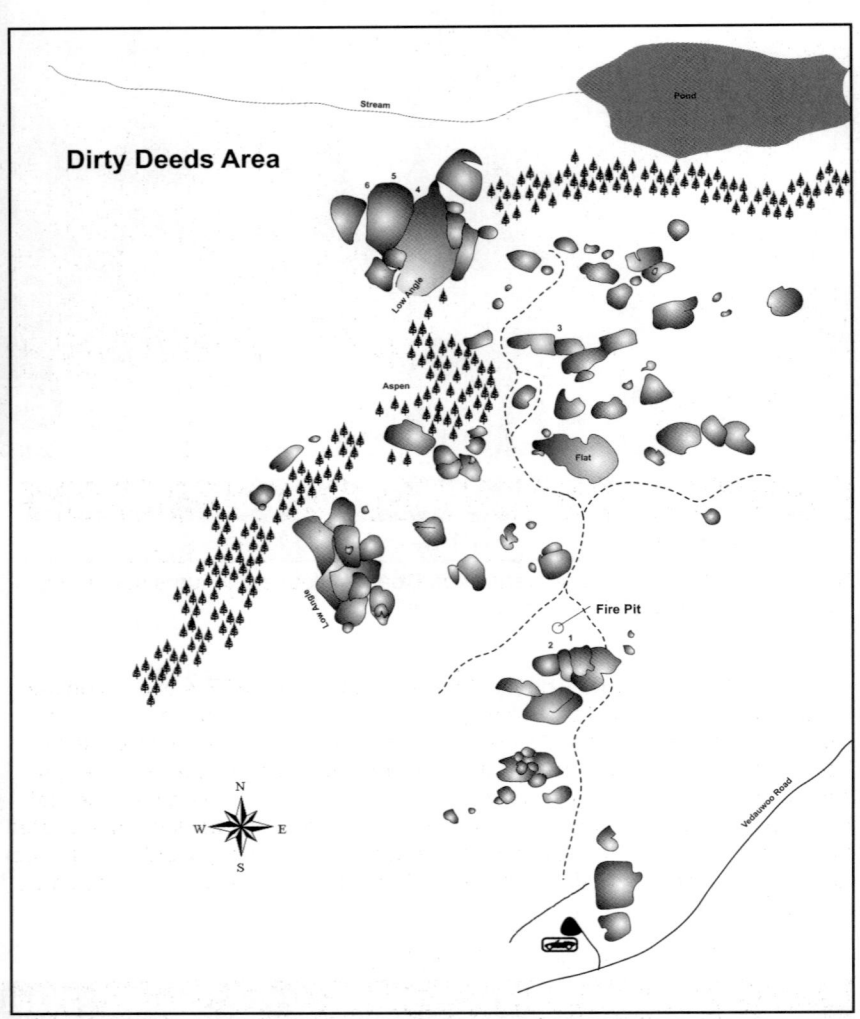

Dirty Deeds Area

Stream

Pond

6 5 4

Low Angle

Aspen

3

Low Angle

Flat

Fire Pit

2 1

N
W E
S

Vedauwoo Road

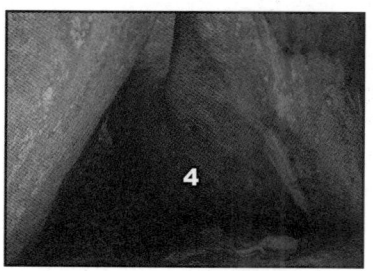

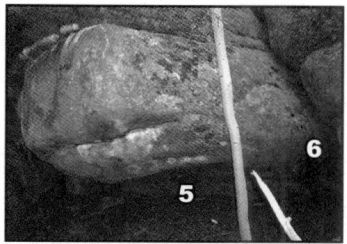

1. 5.10
This is the tall fist and wider crack on the left side of the tall wall. There's a jug up there if you can earn it.
2. 5.11-
This is the wide crack on the right side of the tall wall.
3. 5.9
Sit start the hand crack and traverse left into a wider top with good feet. This is a decent warm up for other cracks in the area.
4. Dirty Deeds 5.12a
Overhanging hand to finger crack in the a-frame of big boulders. Sit start the problem with hands in the pod.
5. V7
Height dependent. Long moves. The obvious roof on flakes just right of the previous problem.
6. 5.11
The a-frame roof crack on the right end of the formation.

Dirty Deeds

To the Moon Alice

	Area Name	Mileage	Turns*
7	Moon/Alice	1.8	11th Left

*From exit 329 head East on Vedauwoo Road. Mileage and turns start from where Vedauwoo Road turns to dirt.

Directions

Located on the left side of Vedauwoo Road after the left turn 700Q and before the left turn 700M, is a pull out up a small rise with boulders on it's crest and flanks. The pull out makes a loop up the hill and down again, around a smaller, split boulder.

1. To The Moon 5.10

The loop road isolates this problem from the larger rocks to the north. Facing the parking area is a widening crack that splits the boulder. Start on comfortable jams down low. Then wedge into the wide stuff.

2. Alice 5.11b

From the parking area, walk around the west end of the rocks and down a hill. This tall crack is just on the right as you reach the northwest facing side of the formation. Tight hands down low lead to flared jams higher up. Some use a toprope on this one.

Problem Distribution Table

	V0-V3	V4-V7	V8-V10	V11+	Cracks	Total
Quantity	0	0	0	0	2	2

The Groove Cartel

Check out the **Debut Album**

"Always Be Closing"

For tour dates, audio clips, and cd info

Go To . . .

TheGrooveCartel.Com

Opposite: Josh Helke on Mullets and Monster Trucks.
Photo: Davin Bagdonas.

Citadel

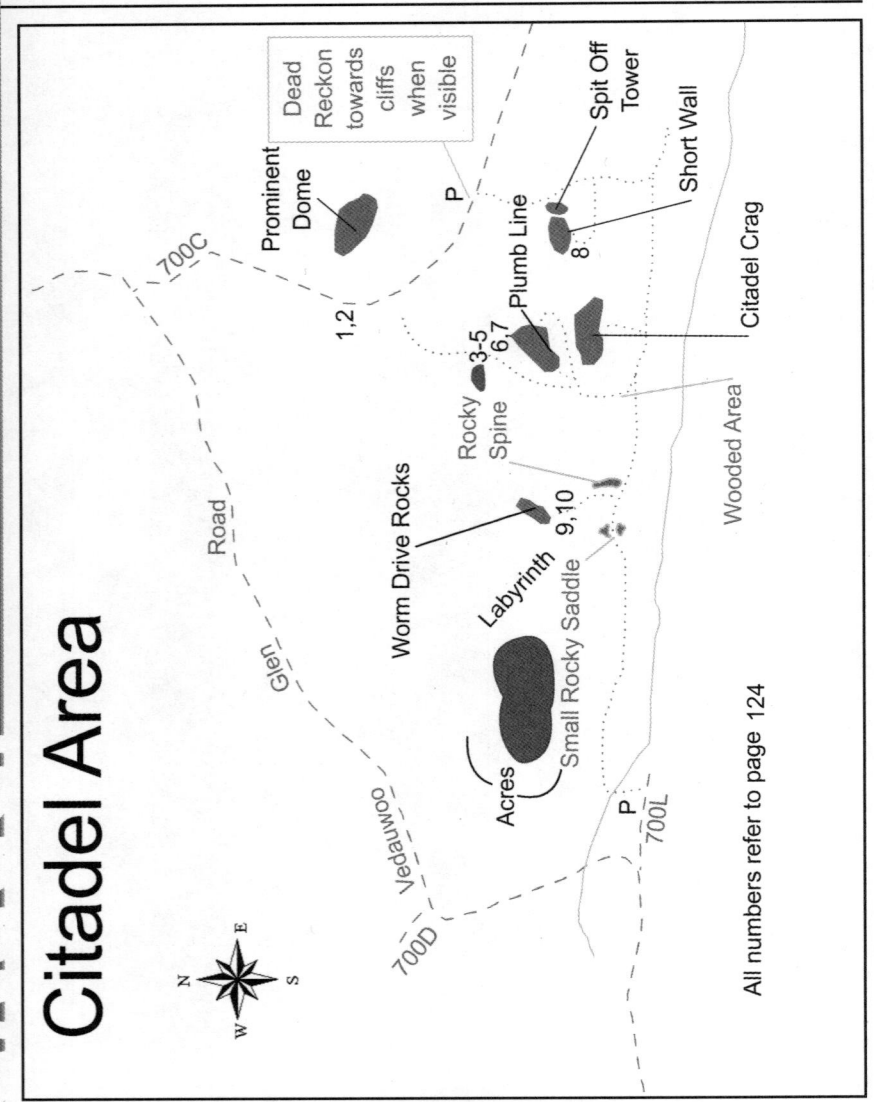

Citadel Area

Citadel

Dead Reckon towards cliffs when visible

Prominent Dome

700C

1,2

P

Spit Off Tower

Short Wall

Plumb Line

8

3-5

6,7

Rocky Spine

Citadel Crag

Wooded Area

Road

Glen

Worm Drive Rocks

9,10

Labyrinth

Vedauwoo

Acres

Small Rocky Saddle

P

700L

700D

N
E
S
W

All numbers refer to page 124

Citadel

	Area Name	Mileage	Turns*
8	Citadel	2	5th Right

*From exit 329 head East on Vedauwoo Road. Mileage and turns start from where Vedauwoo Road turns to dirt.

Problem Distribution Table

	V0-V3	V4-V7	V8-V10	V11+	Cracks	Total
Quantity	35	27	10	0	10	101

*Total includes projects and unrated problems.

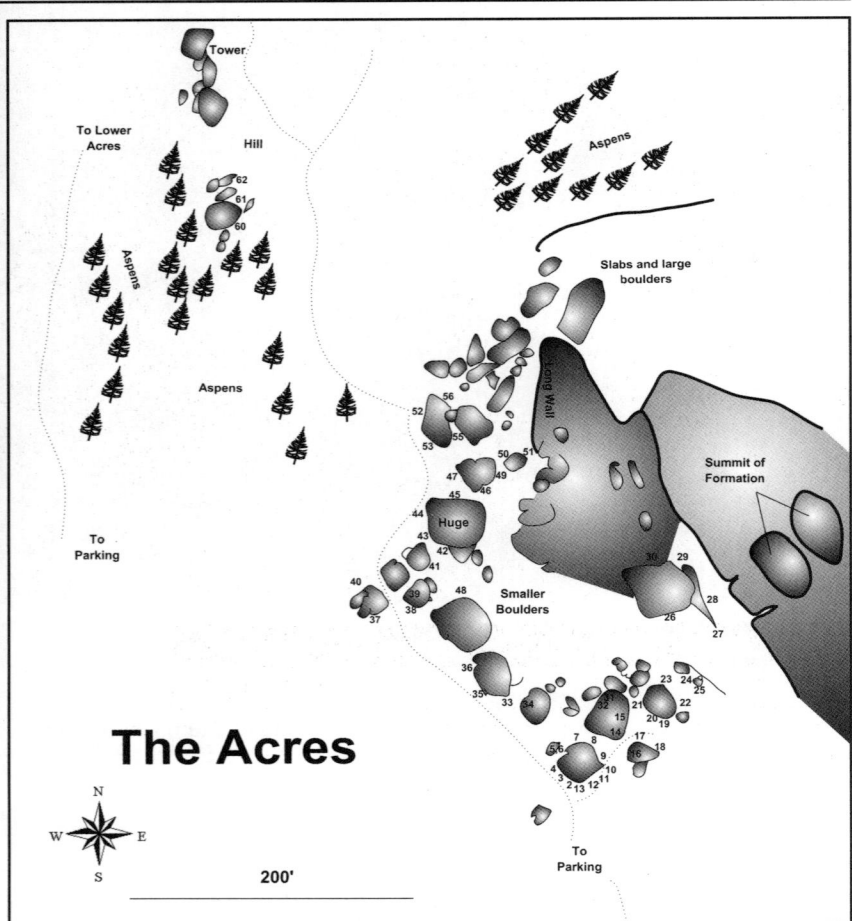

The Acres

N
W — E
S

200'

The Acres
The Bigger Girl Boulder
1. Water Music V3
Start on the big flake. Move right to the arete and follow it to the top. This problem is first seen on the left side

of the trail on the way up the hill from the stream. It is not on the map.
2. Erotic States of Mind V6
Start on the stack of three cobbles on the right side of the dish. Go straight

up to more cobbles on the vertical face.

3. Scared Money Can't Win V5

As of this writing it is unrepeated. Start on the lowest big cobble. Move up into the dish using more cobbles and balance then go left to the prow of the boulder were there are still more cobbles.

4. V8

Mantle the incut cobble and climb the prow.

5. V6

Start on the lowest jug of the left leaning seam. Follow it left and finish by going straight up where the seam ends.

6. V5

Start on a right incut, small cobble and a left sloper. Go straight up.

7. The Home Maker V6

The prow on patina and cobbles.

8. Project

This is the crimpy patina face that is slightly overhanging.

9. Barbed Wire V6

Start on the high crimp/match. Go up to the obvious sloper cobble and finish straight up. Don't remove the wire on the tree. It is part of the problem.

10. V3

Start on the huge cobble and go up the crumbly prow.

11. V4

Start as you do the previous problem but move left into the dish after the cobble is dealt with.

12. The Generic Scoop V3

Jump start to the cobbles in the

scoop. Move left into the dish.

13. Project
Climb the prow right of Erotic States of Mind.

14. The Tipping Point V4
Start standing on the log. Go straight up the very tall prow of the Big Girl Boulder. Hasn't been topped out yet.

15. 12b Toprope

16. The Birth Simulator V2
Start sitting in the bush on the lower lip of the boulder. Go up to the upper lip and mantle.

17. V2
Start on the good cobble down low. V4 if you double dyno.

18. Mr. T V6
Start on the poor, sloping cobble on the left side of the face. The textured top offers a variety of holds to shoot for.

19. Organic V1
The slab on cobbles.

20. V1
Start just left of Organic on a good flake foot and finish on the cobbles of the previous problem.

21. V3
The far left side of the slab. Start on the big inclusion and go up the slab.

22. Straight Line for a Queer Guy V6
Lieback flake with a cobble foot lead to a crystal covered slab.

23. V1
The slab with a lone small inclusion in the middle of the face.

24. Project

25. V5
Start on the cobble under the cap/chock stone and move right and up on more cobbles.

26. V6/7
The tall patina face. Follow incut flakes to the square hold just below the lip of the boulder for a V6/7. After that it's a project.

27. V4
The arete.

28. V0-V2
There are several variations of the slab that is also the down climb.

29. Happy Days V2
The tall slab.

30. V8?
Start on two crimps at the lip of the roof with a good heel hook out right. Move to the flake and up on crimps. Mantle the rail to turn the slab. The flake has broken some and is since unrepeated.

31. V5
Start on the blocky inclusion, move to a smaller inclusion, and then left to the prow to do this problem.

32. Project
Mantle cobble over deadly hole landing.

33. V8
Start with your right in the vertically oriented crimp in the seam and your left on a pinch on the arete. Go up the inside of the dihedral, just right of the prow.

34. V2
Start on an inclusion at mid height and a high foot. Jump start to the big

inclusion near the lip of the boulder.

35. V7
Start on the wind blown pocket/edge. Move slightly right along the way to the top of the undercut boulder.

36. Project
The crack with really poor feet.

37. Chatter Box Project
Follow the diagonaling inclusions until the orange blob is reached. Start on the low end of the diagonal then follow it right. Really sharp.

38. Dust V5
Start low on the vertical inclusion, pinch. Move right.

39. V3
Traverse the lip of the overhanging boulder from right to left and mantle for a good warm up.

40. Corner Mantle V4
Cobble mantle on the prow. Jump off or finish the slab.

41. Hypertrophy Abductorlongus V3 or project
The tall arete to the bucket. It has not been topped out yet.

42. High Ball Mantle V?
Start standing on the rock under the big boulder.

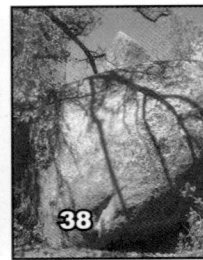

43. John's Crazy Slab V2
Start on the cobbles which might be loose, under the lip of the roof. Take the line of least resistance up the 40 foot slab. John Hennings down climbed the same line after the first ascent.

44. The Exfoliating Bulb V8?
Start on the big, prominent bulb in the big roof. Holds have broken in the roof after that, so gaining the lip is will be difficult.

45. Peanut Butter Conspiracy is Spreading V5
Start high on the sloping seam. Follow the seam left and finish up the sloping arete.

46. V7/8
Start on the undercling in the back of the roof. Go out to a triangle pinch and finish up the arete.

47. V0
Intrusions up the prow.

48. Justin's Mantle V1
The lone cobble above the log.

49. V3 or V8
Start on a left, chest high pinch cobble and a right circular, patina crimp. Go up. The V8 starts on the split/incut cobble in the roof and moves left into the V3.

50. Electric Relaxation V8/9
Sit start on a left gaston in the seam and a right gaston on the horizontal. Throw right to the slimper and move into the hollow flake. Follow the mini dihedral and not the arete to finish this problem.

51. Three's Company 5.9
Tight hands lead to better jams on this high ball crack.

52. Building Blocks V6
Start on a left cobble and a right pinch. Campus to the small edge and then to the triangle pinch. Blocky jugs finish it so don't be a wimp, top it out. 1 pad only.

53. V0
Crystally flake start that leads left to finish on the inclusion.

54. V3
Start on the arete with the left and the right on a vertical edge, then go up the arete.

55. The Ice Queen Project
Start on head high crimps and go straight up on tiny crimps and crystals to the "open" spot between the boulders.

56. V3/4
This is the slab with faint cobbles on it.

57. V7/8
Start with your right in the flake and a high right foot. Move to a small Left pinch/nubbin. Then the top.

58. V6
Sit start with a left low crimp and a right gaston. Go left to a small mail slot and finish on the jug on the right apex of the boulder.

59. Mathematics V8
Sit start on a left low cobble and a lower right sloping edge. Go straight up avoiding the good edge out right, near the chock stone.

60. V5
Start under the butt crease and mantle straight out.

61. V3
Grab the right leaning arete of the boulder and finish at the apex.

62. V1
Start with a left on the arete and the right on a low side pull. Climb the arete to a slightly harder top out.

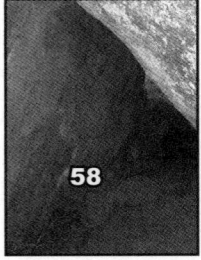

citadel

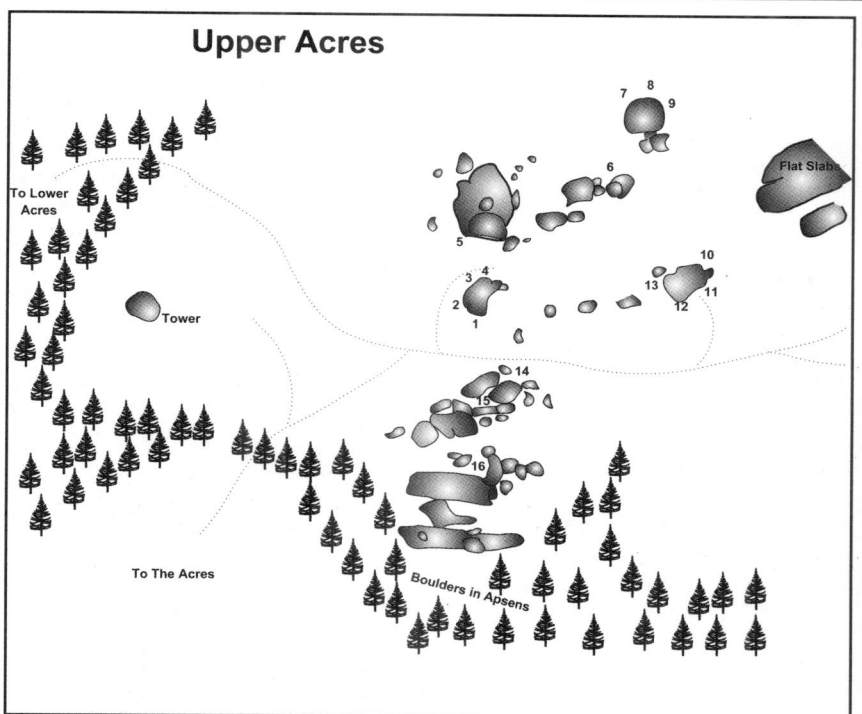

The Upper Acres

The Knot Boulder

1. V4-V6
Sit start on the low incut cobble on the lowest end of the boulder, under the roof. Chuck to the incut at the lip. This problem is height dependent.

2. V0-V3
Good cobbles straight up the boulder (V0), or follow them left all the way to the apex of the boulder (V3).

3. Project
On the gentle overhang, start on the poor sloper cobble. Go up on small stuff.

4. Yellow V7/8
Start with a right on the cobble around the arete and a left in the seam under the overhang. Climb the seam and arete up the overhang to a dyno up high.

5. V0-V?
This is the highly featured face covered in cobbles. Good warm up.

6. Josh's Dyno V4
Go from the low cobble on the lower boulder to the cobble on the higher boulder and mantle. Height dependent.

7. The Nipple Man V8
Sit start the undercling inclusion. Move to the crystal covered face with some smaller inclusions.

8. Violet V3
Start in a left facing lieback, jug, inclusion. Go to cobbles up and right.

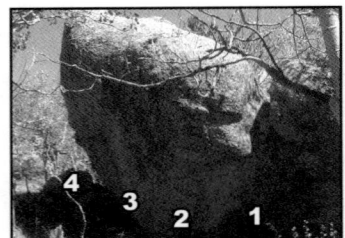

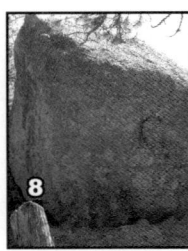

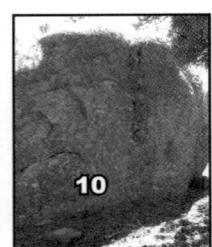

9. V0
Start on a right hand jug on the arete and a good foot. Climb the obvious jugs and chicken heads. Beware of the top. It is loose.

10. V0
The featured back of the boulder.

11. Mullets and Monster Trucks V8
Start left on the crimp/pinch inclusion and right on nothing much. Doesn't matter because you jump start to the cobbles on the vertical face. Top out straight up avoiding scoop to the right. Easier if taller.

12. V4
Start with a high left foot and slopers on the prow. Go up seams and the prow.

13. V0
Start on the huge foot. Take the inclusions for a ride.

14. The Who V9?
Start on the big inclusion in the roof. Move left on a gaston and follow incut flakes farther left to the cruxy, crystally finish. One hold broke so a new sequence may be needed.

15. Project
Football pinch start to some slopers.

16. V3
Take inclusions up and a bit left on the big slab. Start on the small boulder in front of the slab.

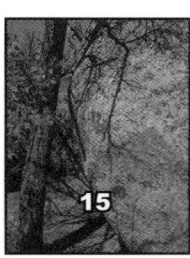

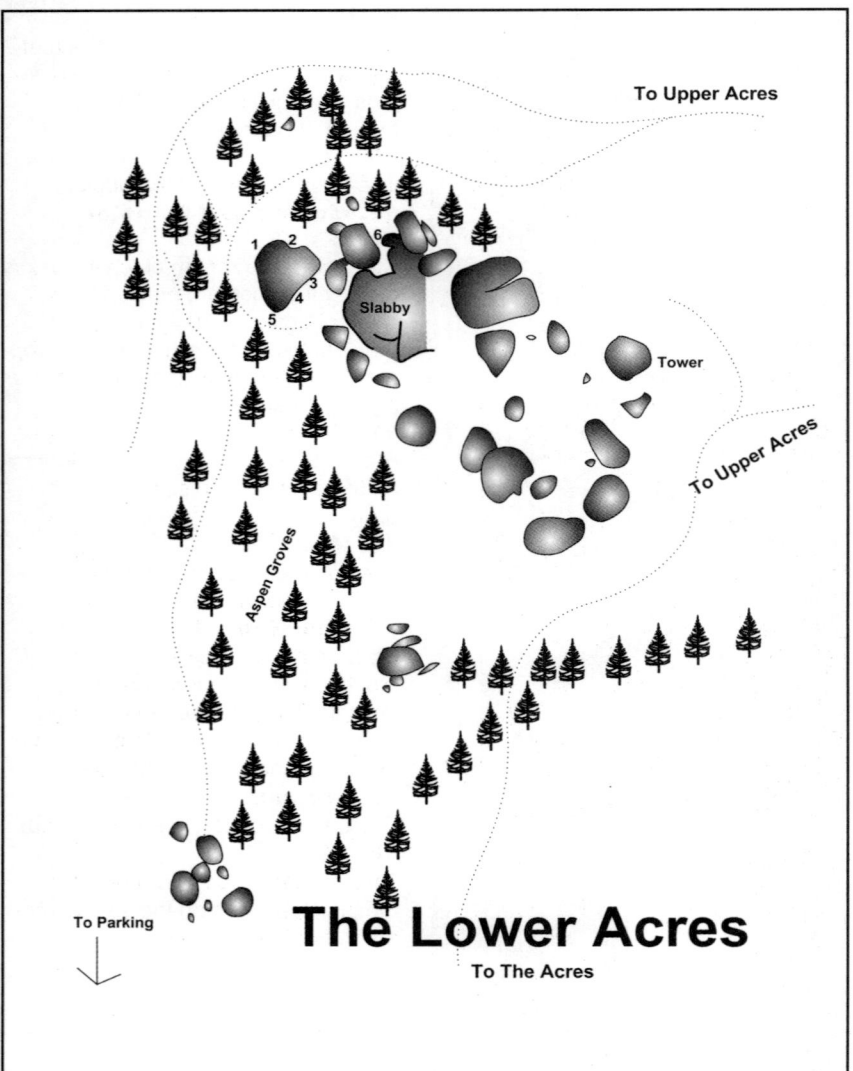

To Upper Acres

1 2 6

3

4 Slabby

5

Tower

To Upper Acres

Aspen Groves

To Parking

The Lower Acres

To The Acres

Citadel

1. The Generic Font Problem
V2

Climb cool slopers to the top.

2. V4

Climb the dihedral.

3. Slab Project

4. V5

Bright pink blank slab.

5. V0

Climb the blunt, low angle nose. This problem is also the down climb for this boulder.

6. V7

Start on loose flakes under roof, throw to lip then follow arete to top.

Citadel

Josh Helke on Cream Puff.
Photo: Davin Bagdonas.

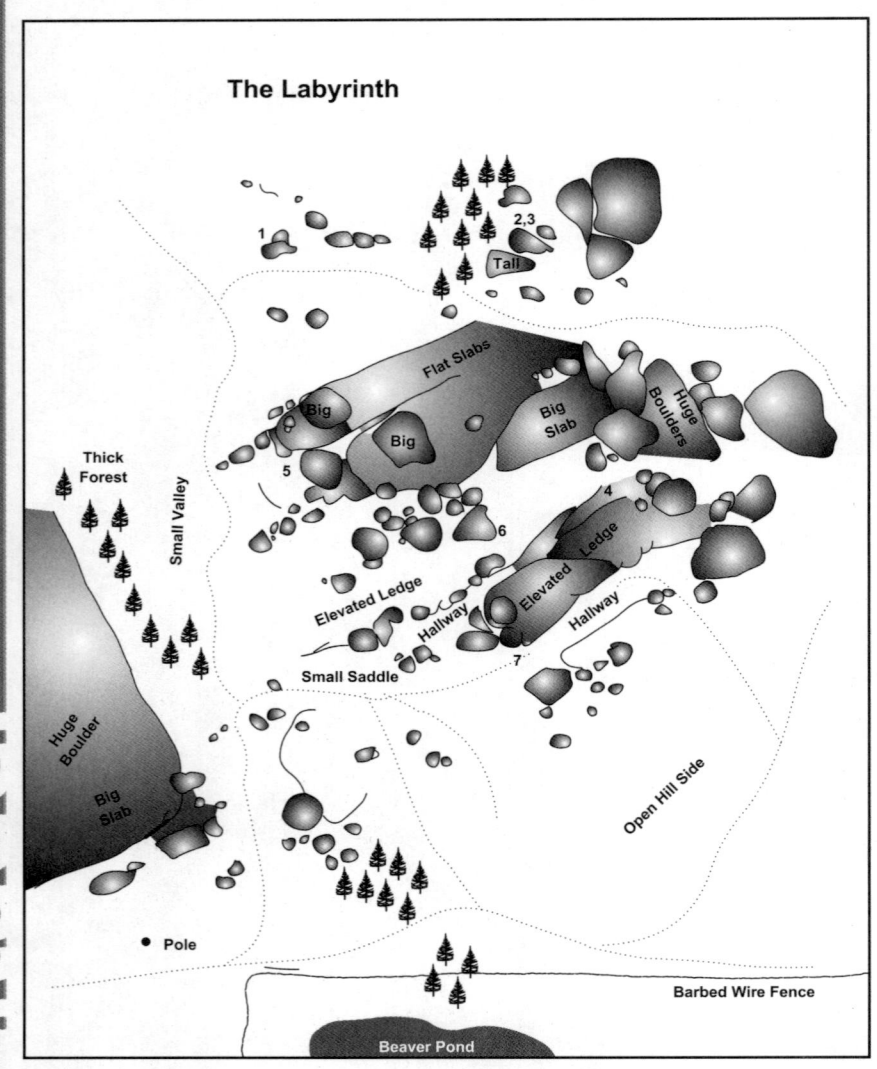

The Labyrinth

The Labyrinth

1. A Much Better Tomorrow V4

Start under the roof on a good mail slot rail. Pull to the next rail up and the cobble above.

2. Puddin' V6

Sit start on the lowest good cobble and undercling with feet on the crumbly rock. Straight up on the cobbles to the sloping top.

3. Cream Puff V8

Same start as the previous problem, but go right along the cobbles to the last high cobble and pull for the apex of the sloping top.

4. V5

The small sloping edges up the vertical wall.

5. Project

The tall patina face on crisp crimps. Could be done as a sit start or a stand start. Both ways are projects.

6. V2

The slab with a small cobble for the toes. Hard to convince yourself to leave the cobble's safety.

7. 5.11a

Short roof crack that turns to a vertical face.

and jam under where the two boulders touch, going for the wide crack about ten feet off the deck. The start in the lower cave is a project linkup.

4. 5.11b
Hands to tight hands to finger tips at the exit of the right leaning crack.

5. 5.8
The hand crack flake. Good!

6. 5.11a
The right exit roof problem under the giant "chock stone".

7. 5.11c
The left exit roof problem under the giant "chock stone".

8. The Tax Man 5.11d
The tight hands roof about ten feet off the deck. It is just to the west of the short wall, on the short wall's end. Very classic, very scary.

9. Where the Wild Things Are V 5.12d
A tall left leaning splitter. Begins as steep, tight hands then goes to fingers and perfect hands higher up. Ends on a ledge about 20 feet up, but ten more feet of climbing is needed to escape the ledge.

10. Eight Ounces to Freedom V 5.13a
A ten foot, left facing dihedral roof crack. Stat on hands then move into fists, followed by offwidth moves around the lip. There are some hand jams around the chock stone for the finish.

The Citadel Proper

1. 5.6
The short vertical hand crack.

2. 5.7
This is the left start to the previous problem, on a right leaning crack that intersects the vertical crack.

3. Legend of Sleepy Hollow 5.12b
This problem is located under where two very large boulders meet at the end of the meadow and in front of a taller formation. Start on face moves

Opposite: Liz Hajek on Problem 5.
Photo: Davin Bagdonas

Opposite: Dave Nash on The Third Finger.
Photo: Matt Williams.

Gallery

Liz Hajek on The Ice Queen Project at the Citadel.
Photo: Ken Driese.

Clint Cook on Shin and Bones, V3 at the Bunker.
Photo: Davin Bagdonas.

Erik Christensen on Suzuki Roof. Photo: Josh Helke.

ORGANIC

BOULDERING MATS

art needs inspiration

inspiration needs a *source*

www.organicclimbing.com
quality crash pads & bouldering gear

a. raether, good vibrations, vedauwoo - heilke photo

Bob Scarpelli on Alice.
Photo: Zach Orenczak.

Bob Scarpelli on a
"Vedauwoo Walk Off".
Photo: Rachael Lynn.

Cody Ramsey on the Tempest, V10 at the Nautilus.
Photo: Matt Williams

Trevor Turmelle on Iron Maiden.
Photo: Ken Driese

Andy Raether on The Borg, V11 In Central.
Photo: Davin Bagdonas

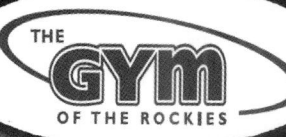

INDOOR ROCK CLIMBING

FEATURING

~ 6200 Sq. Ft. of Textured Terrain
~ 1000 Sq. Ft. Free Standing Boulder
~ 750 Sq. Ft. CAVE
~ Adjoining Multi-Sports Complex

~ Group Rates
~ Instruction
~ Rental Gear
~ Private Lessons
~ Summer Camps
~ Competitions

COME CLIMB THE BEST IN FORT COLLINS

970~221~5000

1800 Heath Pkwy ~ Fort Collins CO ~ 80524

www.thegymoftherockies.com

Justin Edl on Desiderata, 5.12d, Central.
Photo: Davin Bagdonas

**Mike Helke on Problem 57, V7, in the Citadel.
Photo: Josh Helke**

Opposite: Clint Cook on problem 11, V3, Closely spotted by Bevan Frost.
Photo: Davin Bagdonas.

Coyote Rocks

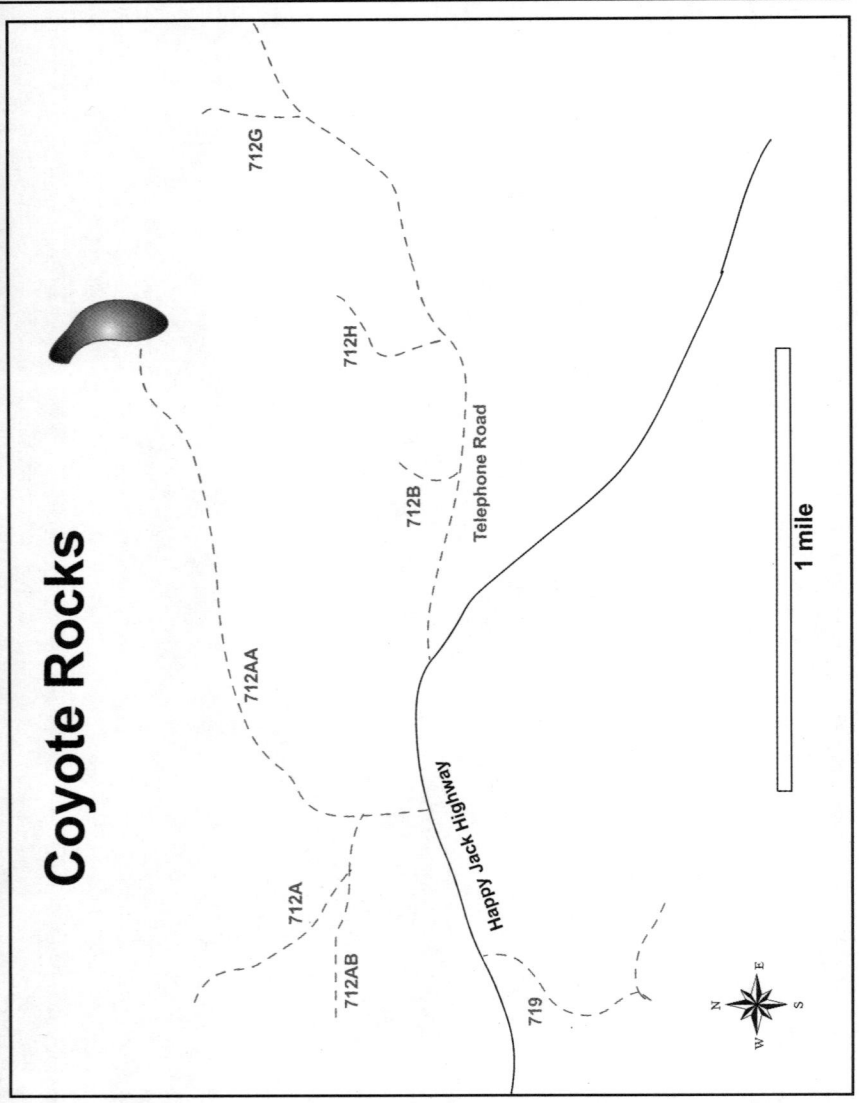

Coyote Rocks

712G

712H

Telephone Road

712B

712AA

Happy Jack Highway

712A

712AB

719

1 mile

N
W   E
S

Coyote Rocks

	Area Name	Mileage	Turns*
9	Coyote Rocks	2.3	2nd Left

*From exit 323 turn on to Happy Jack road. Mileage and turns begin when you turn on to Happy Jack Road.

Directions

From the Happy Jack Exit, take Happy Jack Highway for 2.3 miles. Turn on the second left onto road 712A. Bear right on road 712AA to the end. Navigating to the boulders is at first difficult but once you make it to the rocks it will be easy to find your way around.

Problem Distribution Table

	V0-V3	V4-V7	V8-V10	V11+	Cracks	Total*
Quantity	19	17	4	0	4	45

*Total includes projects and unrated problems.

143

Erik Christensen cranks through the Acid House, V6.
Photo: Josh Helke

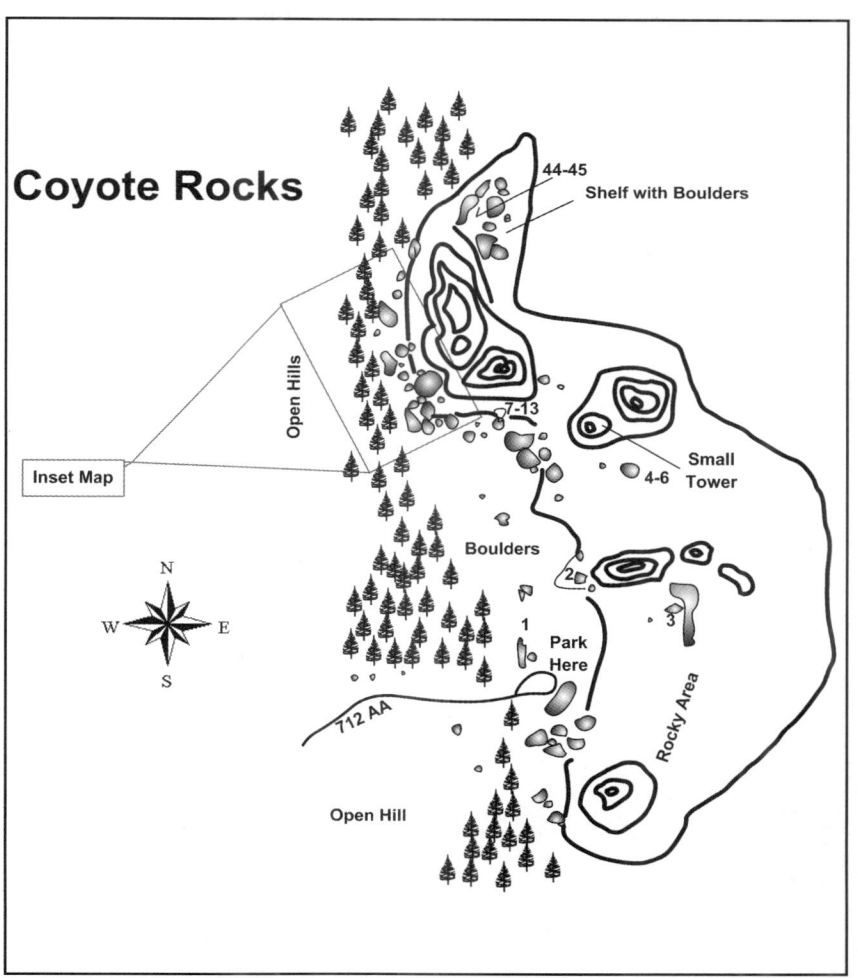

Coyote Rocks

44-45
Shelf with Boulders

Open Hills

Inset Map

7-13

Small
Tower

4-6

Boulders

N
W — E
S

2

3

1
Park
Here

712 AA

Rocky Area

Open Hill

1. The Camp Trick V2
Just a short walk from the parking lot, hang start the beak and mantle directly over the tip.

2. The Zit V3
Jump start to the smooth, one hand bulb, and go on up.

3. Bottle of Nothing V4
Sit start the gentle overhanging bulge on a crimp and sloping side pull.

4. Acid House V6
Sloping roof problem located over the back of the formation from the parking lot. Can be done from the back of the roof or down and left. Either way, climb out the roof on slopers.

5. La Ventana Del Sol V4
Hand crack roof.

6. Fading Light V2
Climb the slab .

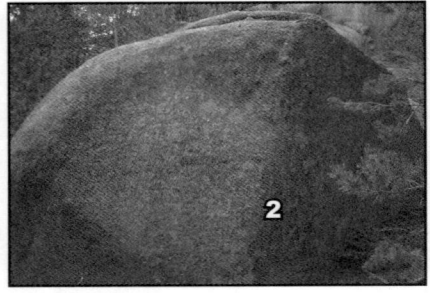

Coyote Rocks

146

Coyote Rocks

7. V1
Lieback seams to start the problem, then move up on crimps.

8. Pokey Little Pine V3
Use sloping edges up the face on the left end of the boulder where the little pine goes through the gap.

9. Don't be Creepy V2
Diagonal undercling then crimps.

10. Meridians of Passion V9
Start on the toothy edge at waist level, under the bulge. Pull crimpers to the diagonal rail and finish on the rounded top.

11. V3
Start on the low, sloping end of the boulder, lip traverse to the arete and mantle up.

12. Stings Like a Bee V4
On the left end of the boulder use seams to start, then move up on crystals and the horizontal seam, finishing on top.

13. V2
Go up on the horizontal seam.

14. V3
Starting on the obvious edge in the middle of the boulder, move straight up to crystals and crimps.

15. Slick Slab Right V2
Good feet on the dish take you to small edges and slopers.

16. Slick Slab Left V3
Small crimps to a sloping rail and up.

17. Love Springs Eternal V5
This is the overhanging arete problem located behind some smaller boulders. From the sit start, climb up and right. Starting without the small

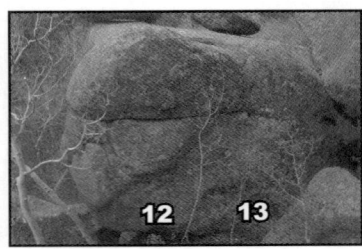

Coyote Rocks

rock under the roof for feet has not been done.

18. Roast Possum Vinegar Pie V5

Start on the lowest sloping dish/lip of the roof and climb out slopers and a crimp at the lip to gain the other side/lip of the roof then mantle.

19. Green Tea V1

Good warm up for the area and the first problem done at Coyote Rocks. Start on the lowest good hold of the seam and go up to good holds and the slabby top out.

20. A Form Like Kata V5

Opposing diagonal crimps to more crimps moving right near the top. Exiting left for the top of the previous problem is an easier variation. The sit start is around V7.

21. SPF V6

Jump or stacked pad start to the good edge. The only problem on the long and gently overhanging face.

22. Project

The tall overhanging face of the Meditation boulder on small crimps! Really hard.

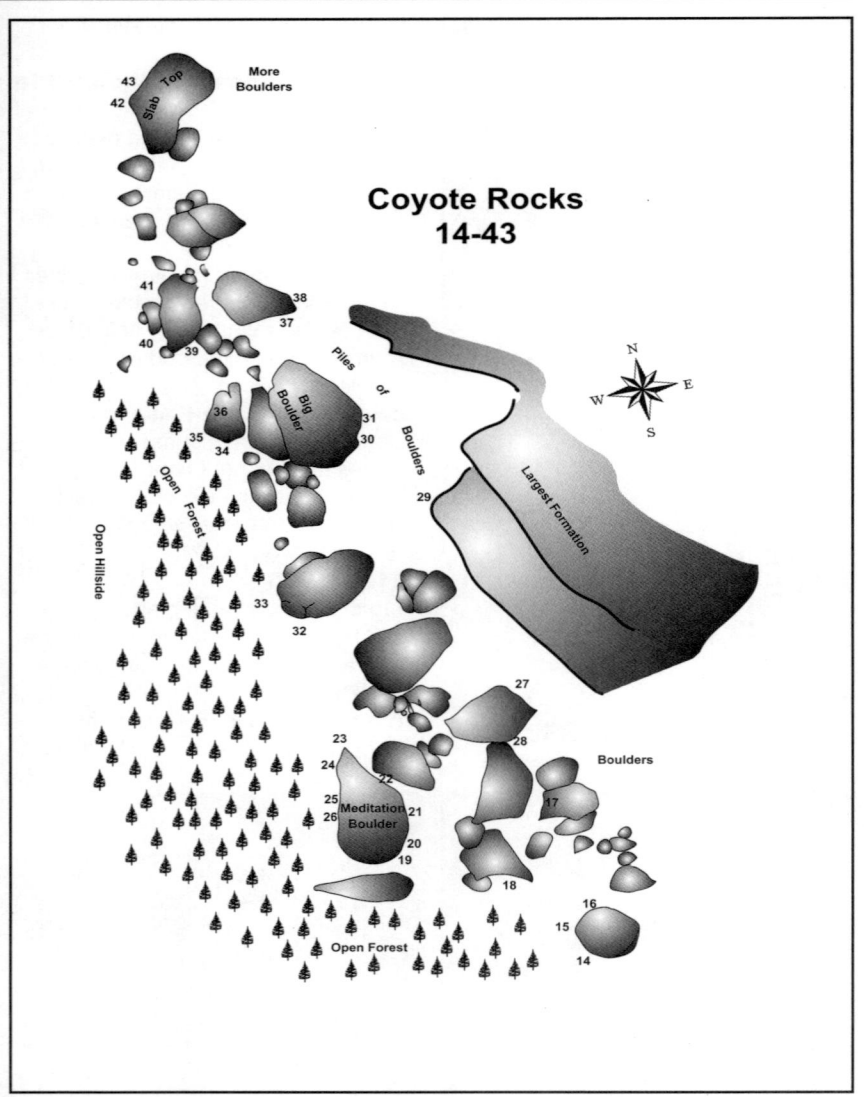

Coyote Rocks
14-43

23. Short Bus V8
The arete.
24. Black Tea V4
The left end of the slab where you can still use the arete to start.
25. V6
Start in the middle of the slab on a good edge and finish by going left on crimps and crystals.
26. V7 ?
Same start as the previous problem but goes right and up on bad holds.
27. The Miser V7
Golden patina overhang.
28. Equilibrium V5
Two crimps take you up and left to the seam.
29. Pimp Slap V3
Slopers on the left end of the boulder.
30. The Rose V7
Dihedral problem.
31. The Thorn V8
Same start as the Rose, but go right on crimps after the dihedral.

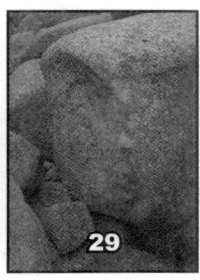

32. 5.7 or 5.9
Sit starting the crack is harder than the stand start.

33. Strangelove V6
A low start flake with bad feet leads to very small crimps on the rounded top.

34. Dead Wood V1
Sit start on the long right leaning rail and mantle over the highest part of the boulder.

35. V4/5
The left prow of the dead wood boulder. Watch the loose chunk.

36. The Glass Slab V0 or T4 (Tennis Shoe 4)
The lowest angle slab in Vedauwoo.

37. V3
The featured face. Start on edges left of the arete.

38. King of Beers V0
Follow clean diagonal edges up the slab.

39. Happy Hour 5.12-
Wide crack roof in the a-frame boulders. Splitter.

40. Heart of Stone V8
The tall, steep face between the two smaller boulders. Sit start on sloping holds and mantle your heart out.
41. V1
Mantle some crimps and finish up the bulge.
42. Rust V5
Begin on broken holds on the low prow of the big boulder right of the aspen trees. Finish with a sketchy mantle on the slab.
43. V2
Jump start to the sloping, but good edge/seam and mantle on up the slab.

Use map on page 145 to locate the following problems.

44. 5.11
Sit start the finger crack that leads to better jams.
45. 5.10
Sit start the hand crack.

Coyote Rocks

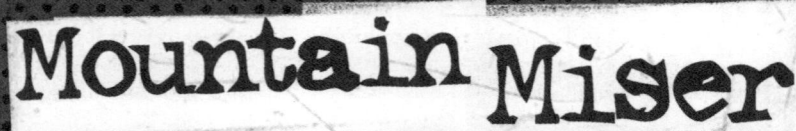

Opposite: Bevan Frost on 7 Levels of Purgatory, V2.
Photo: Davin Bagdonas

Telephone Road

Telephone Road

Telephone Road Boulders

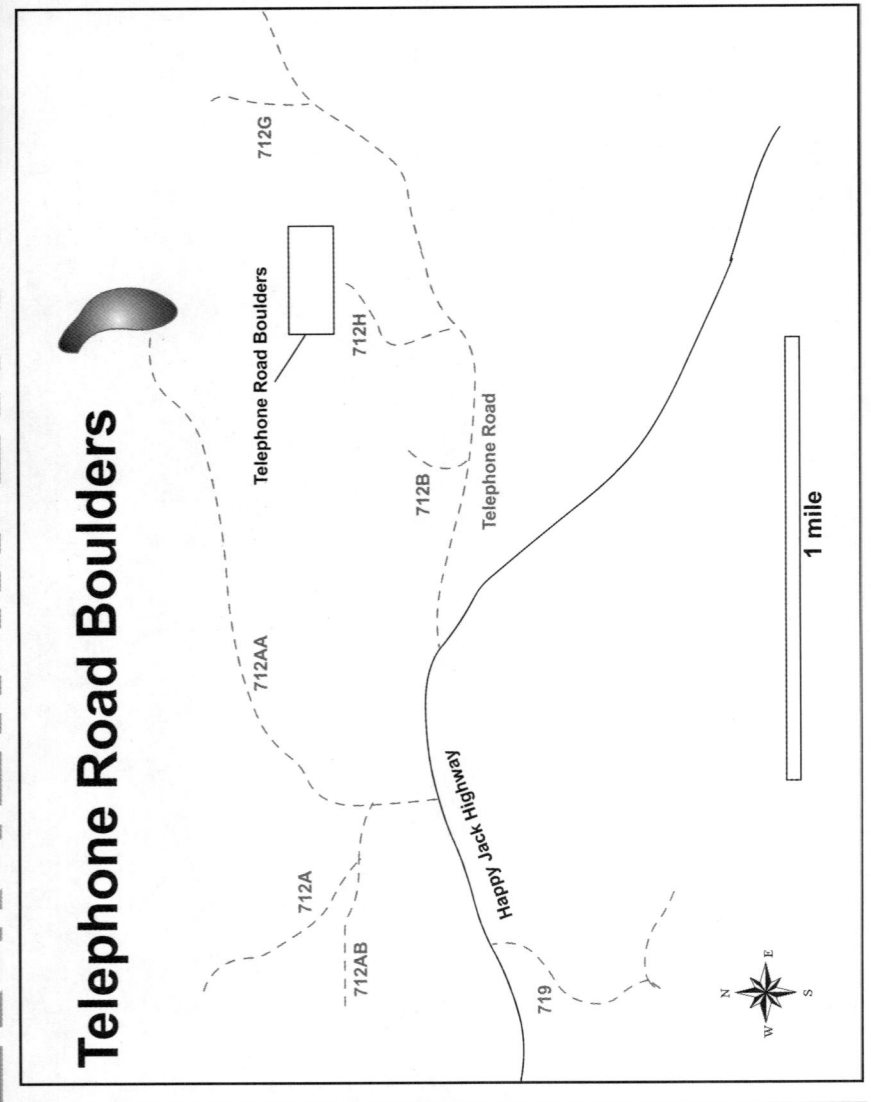

Telephone Road

	Area Name	Mileage	Turns*
10	Telephone Road	2.75	3rd Left

*From exit 323 turn on to Happy Jack road. Mileage and turns begin when you turn on to Happy Jack Road.

Directions

From the Happy Jack Exit of Interstate 80, go 2.75 miles down the Happy Jack Highway to where a turn out is on the right and road 712 is on the left. Take the left turn down 712 and go for another mile. Turn left and down the hill of road 712H and follow it to the bottom parking loop. Across the drainage you will see a couple of smaller rock outcroppings and a large boulder about halfway up the hill. These are the Telephone Road Boulders. There are other problems on the side of the drainage that you are parking on. Go up the hill toward the east and walk into the small rock formations.

Problem Distribution Table

	V0-V3	V4-V7	V8-V10	V11+	Cracks	Total*
Quantity	16	7	0	0	3	29

*Total includes projects and unrated problems.

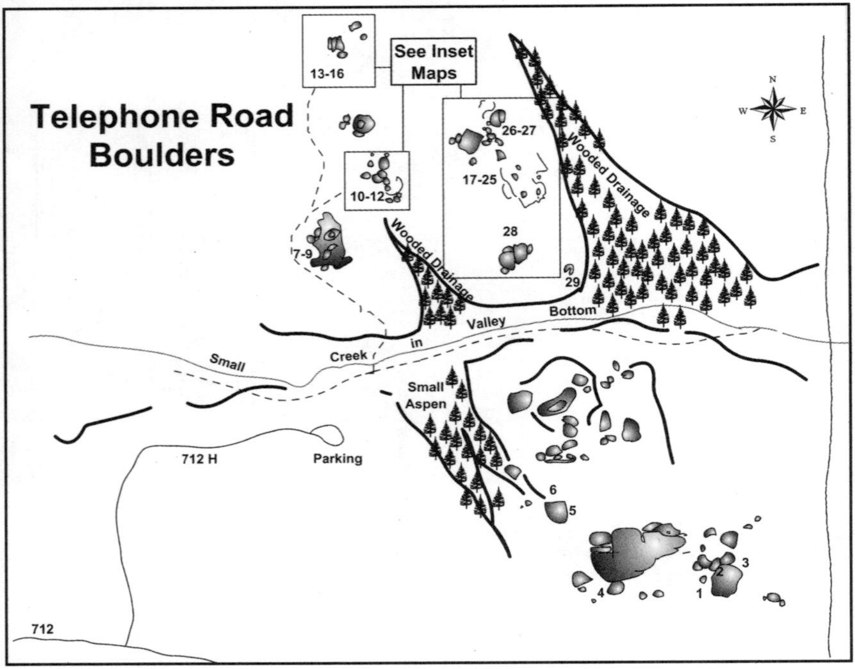

Telephone Road Boulders

See Inset Maps

13-16

10-12

7-9

26-27

17-25

28

29

Wooded Drainage

Wooded Drainage

Valley Bottom

Small Creek in

Small Aspen

712 H

Parking

712

6

5

2

3

1

4

1. Welcome Home V3
Crimps on the left side of the prow.
2. Corinne V2
Climb the slab on crimps and crystals that get thinner near the top.

3. Tuesdays V6
Climb the bulge on the back of the boulder using edges.

4. Project
The finger crack roof with a dike in it. This problem is downhill from the large boulder containing the previous problems.

5. The Egg V3
Use slopers on the right side of the face. Traverse low to the eggs, then up.

6. Triangle Balance V2
Sit start on the right side of the triangular face and use a crimpy side pull to find your balance.

The next problems are described for the hillside across the drainage and uphill from the creek.

7. Go to a Happy Place / Sloppy Seconds V2/3
Under the gentle overhanging wall, sit start on an edge and lieback edge to the right of the vertical seam. Go left to finish on the good holds of the big seam.

8. El Diablo V4
Direct finish to the previous problem (no good holds in the seam).

9. Project V6/7?
Sit start left on a low sloper, make a right side pull and go straight up.

Telephone Road

Telephone Road

10. Thunder Storm Escape V4
Same hueco start as the previous problem, but go left on edges and slopers then mantle the left end of the boulder.

11. Thunder Storm is Coming V3
Sit start in a hueco and move up to the slopey mantle at the top.

12. $150 Secret V4
Low left hand, right hand sloper, and go straight up.

13. Mosquito Face V0
The slab on the east facing side of the boulder.

14. Mosquito Crack 5.10
The off fingers crack.

15. Unnamed 5.6
The short, not as good crack left of the previous problem.

16. Turtle Belly V4
Sit start the turtle shell textured face to slopers on the prow.

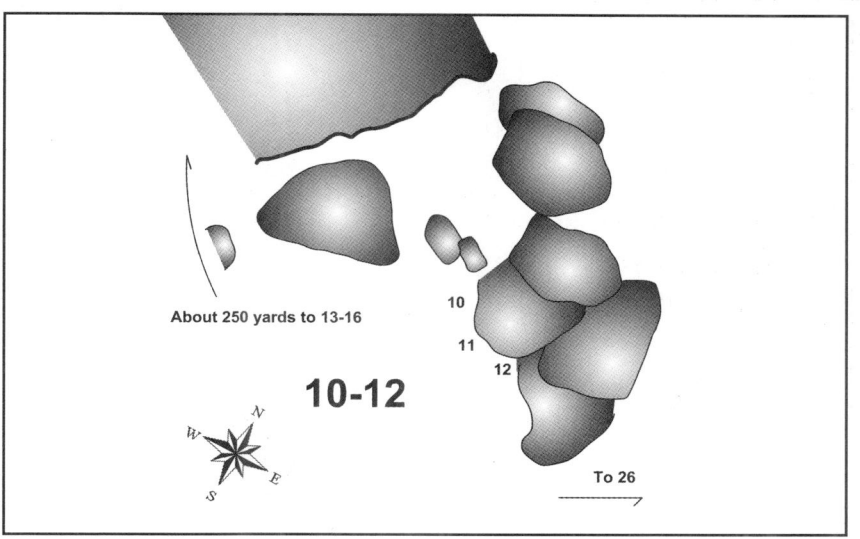

About 250 yards to 13-16

10

11

12

10-12

To 26

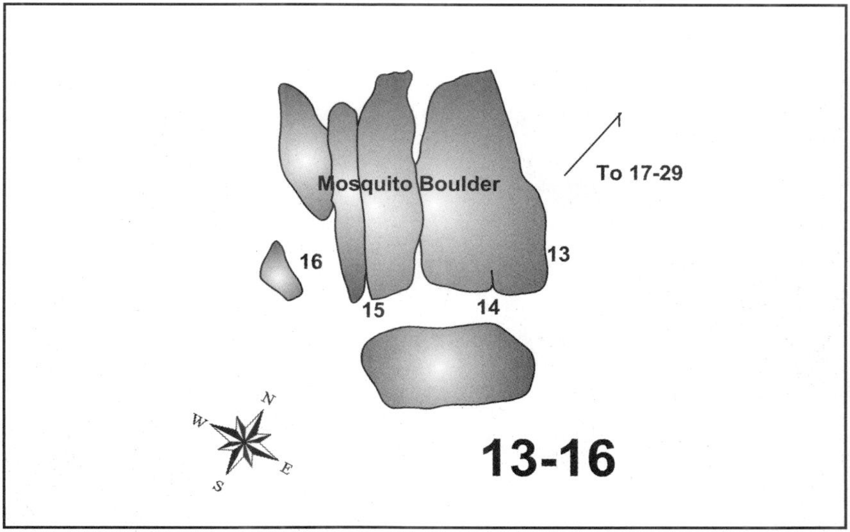

Mosquito Boulder

To 17-29

16

15

14

13

13-16

Telephone Road

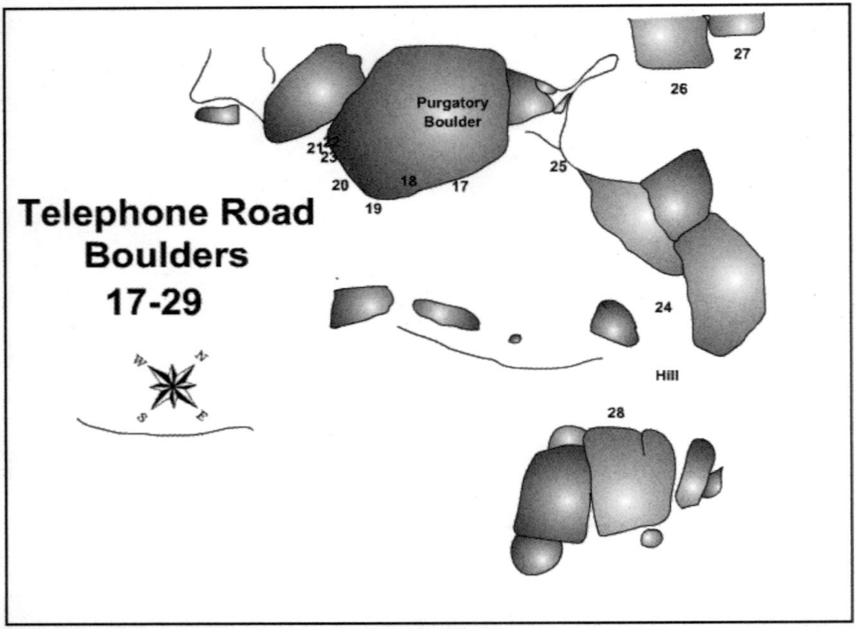
Telephone Road
Boulders
17-29
Purgatory
Boulder
21
22
23
20
19
18
17
25
26
27
24
Hill
28
W
N
S
E

26
27
25
18
17
24
21-23
20
19

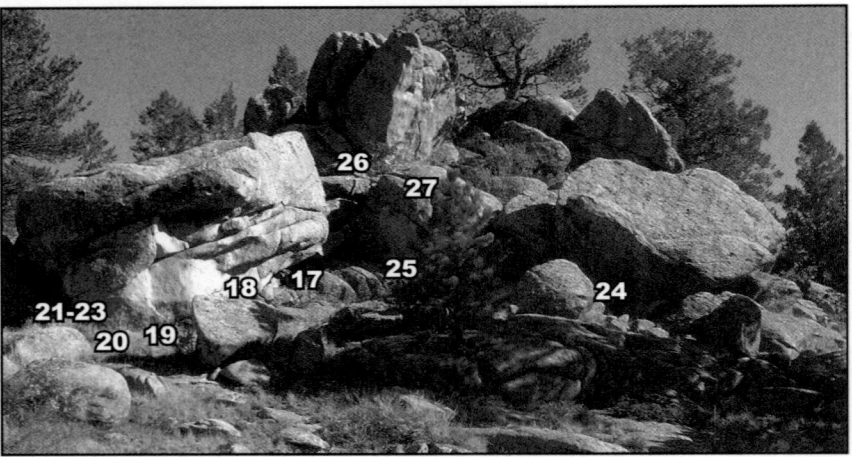

17. Seven Levels of Purgatory V2
Sit start under the roof on a good sloping jug. Move up to the seam under the roof and continue through the levels. This is a great problem.

18. The Annihilator V1
Start just left of the previous problem on good holds. Go up on positive grips.

19. Bristo Cannon V3
Waist high mounds get you motivated for the belly flop top out.

20. Get It Up V3
Start on the undercling, and go for the top using an obvious crimp.

21. Guano Traverse V1
Start just left of the pile of guano and move right from the starting jug along more good jugs.

22. Body Rock Traverse V4
Same start as the previous problem, but stay low on bad holds below the good holds of the previous problem. Finish on the white horn.

23. Needing Something Real V3
Start on a sloper left of problem 18, move into an undercling and finish on problem 17.

24. Jehovah V4
Sit start on the lowest edges of the gentle overhang and gun for the top.

25. Current V2
Lie back the seam looking things.

26. V1
Clean face over a terrible landing.

27. 5.7
Good jamming in a hand crack, but don't fall.

28. Way Up North V2
Sit start the flake on the less than vertical wall.

29. Project
Sit start the finger crack. Basically a one arm pull up on a good lock. (On overview map)

Opposite: Tess McGinty on The Pawn, V2.
Photo: Matt Williams

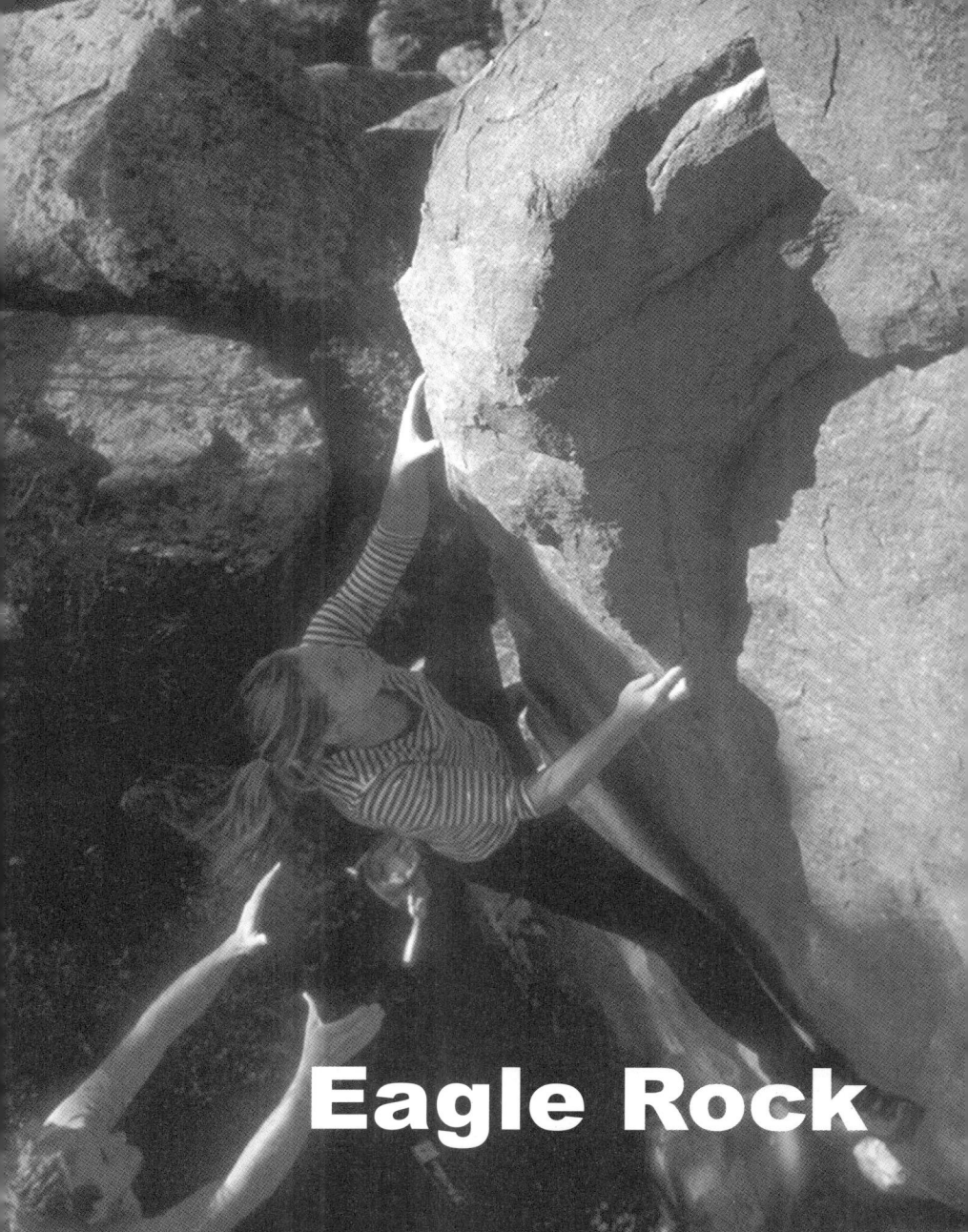

Eagle Rock

Eagle Rock

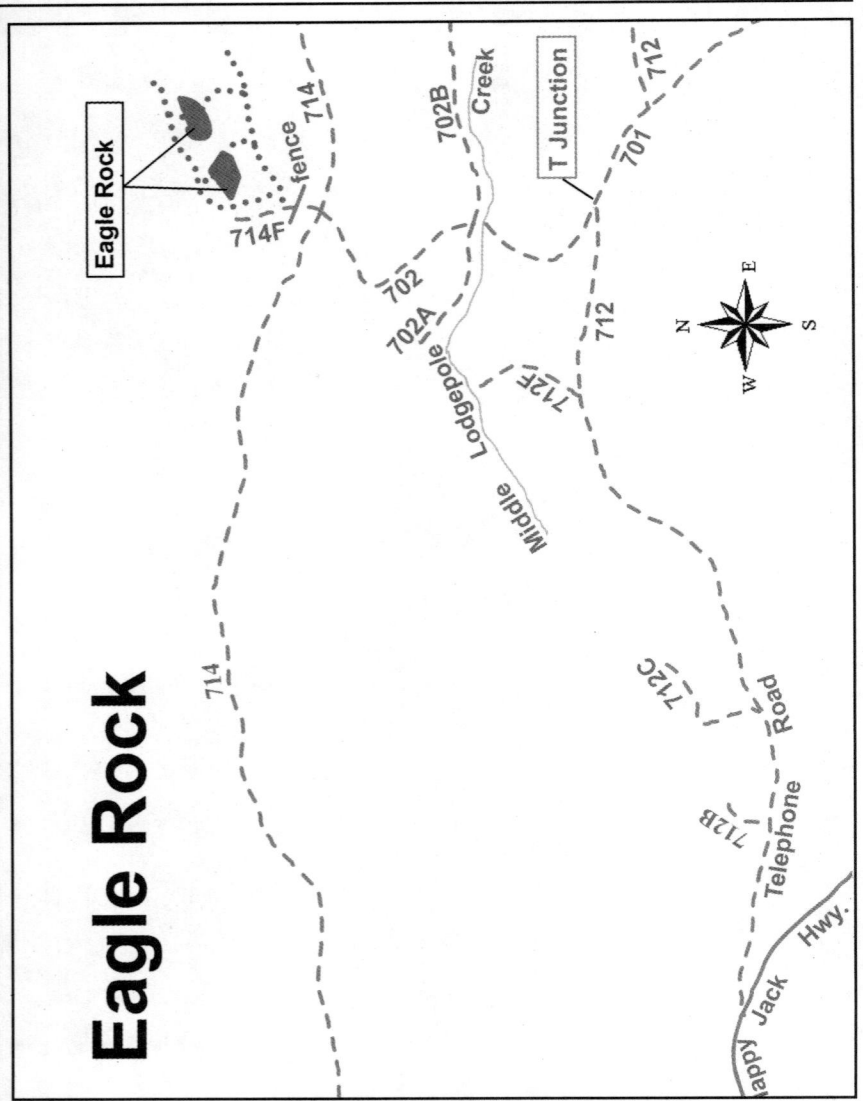

Eagle Rock

	Area Name	Mileage	Turns*
11	Eagle Rocks	2.75	4th Left

*From exit 323 turn on to Happy Jack road. Mileage and turns begin when you turn on to Happy Jack Road.

Directions

Take Happy Jack Highway for about two miles from Interstate 80. Go left on Telephone Road (712). Drive on road 712 until a t-junction is reached, at which point make a left on road 702. Follow, through a drainage and over a hill past a four way intersection. Continue straight through the gate and park at the end of the road under the tall towers of Eagle Rock. The bouldering is divided into three areas: The Nest, Main Eagle Boulders, and The Lower Eagle Boulders.

Directly North and above the parking area is The Nest. It is most easily reached by following the old road up the hill and hanging right when the first tower is reached on the right. The Nest is on the elevated shelf on the West side of the tower.

Problem Distribution Table

	V0-V3	V4-V7	V8-V10	V11+	Cracks	Total*
Quantity	25	18	0	0	2	49

*Total includes projects and unrated problems.

Eagle Rock

The Nest

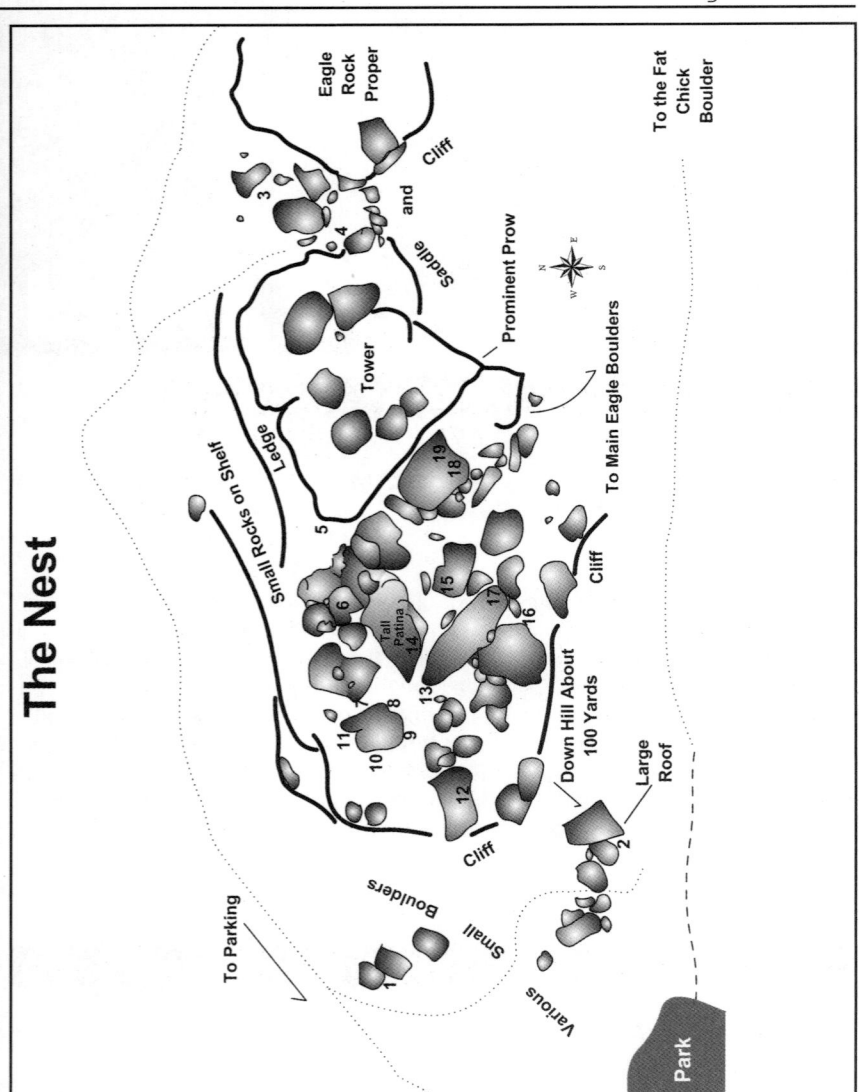

The Main Eagle Boulders are located directly below the tallest formation of Eagle Rock, under the main cliffs. They are concentrated in the thick aspen grove along the trail.

The Lower Eagle Boulders are reached by walking east from the parking area, through the Main Eagle Boulders, and through the thick aspen groves to the eastern most formations of Eagle Rock.

The Nest

1. V1

This problem is located on the right side of the old road and faint trail, about half way up the hill, below The Nest. Sit start edges, up edges on broken blocks.

2. V3

This problem is located just beyond the parking area to the east, on the left side of the trail. It is the prominent roof boulder with a flat dirt landing. Jug in roof to apex/lip of roof and up on the good holds.

3. V5

Start with right hand on the arete in the roof and left on the edge in the roof. There is a good jug at the lip.

4. ?

Good rock on the west/right side of the saddle/gap above the hole.

5. The Pawn V2/3
Sit start the jug and go up the double arete on the West end tower.

6. Cartoony Moon V2
Sit start or stand start the mini dihedral above the smaller boulder.

7. V0
Turtle shell slab over a bad landing in the gap.

8. V2
Start, right hand in the incut, left hand on the bulb, and go up to the horn.

9. Eyeshot V4
The dark colored patina face. It is height dependent so the grade is an average.

10. Patina Face V3-V5
The obvious patina face. The left side using the patina prow is V3. V3 up the middle, and V5 if you sit start right.

11. V0
Crack to patina jugs. Has good sit start.

12. V3
Lie back start in the less than vertical scoop.

13. V0
Sit start this problem on a hand jam for the right and a jug for the left. Move up the prow of the boulder on a jug to slab moves higher up.

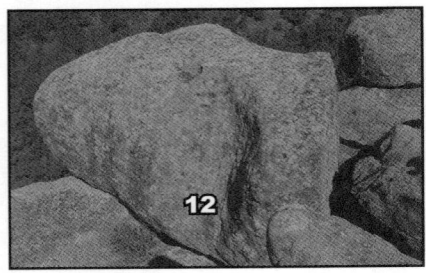

Sit start on the FAR left undercling for the left and an edge for the right. Work edges for the good, blocky hold on the arete and head for the apex of the boulder.

16. V0
Lip traverse warm up.

17. V3/4
Start down in the hole on opposing sloping edges. Go to slopers at the lip of the bottom boulder and pull to the patina face of the upper boulder.

18. V4
Start on crimps on the rail on the left side of the black face. Pull all the way to the lip.

19. V6
Dyno from the sloping rail to the lip of the boulder.

14. Project
The right leaning splitter crack in the corridor. It moves out the corridor and goes up the patina face. Just opposite of 15.

15. That Way Madness Lies V7
The overhanging patina face in the pit at the back/East end of the corridor.

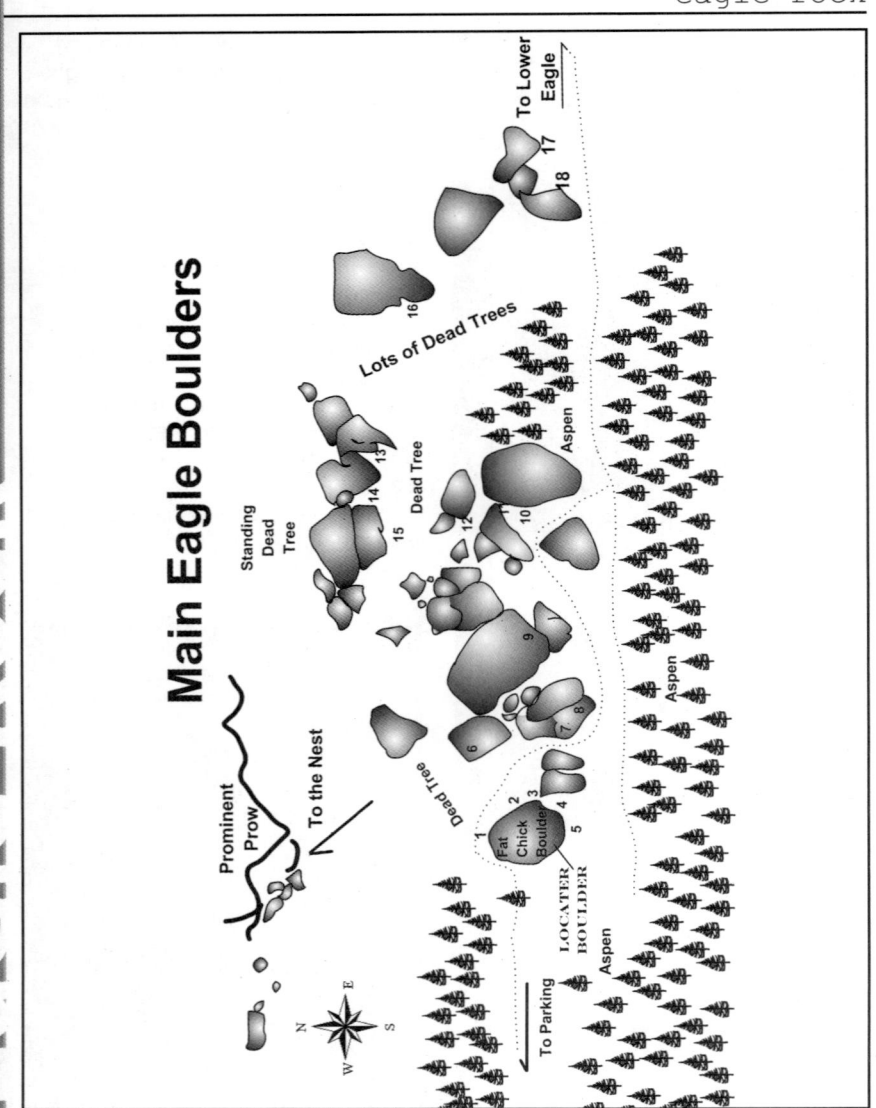

Main Eagle Boulders

Prominent Prow

To the Nest

Standing Dead Tree

Dead Tree

Lots of Dead Trees

To Lower Eagle

17
18
16
13
14
15
12
10
9
8
7
6
5
4
3
2
1

Dead Tree

Fat Chick Boulder

LOCATER BOULDER

Aspen

Aspen

Aspen

To Parking

N
E
S
W

Eagle Rock

Main Eagle Boulders

The Fat Chic Boulder

1. V0
Sloper, rising, lip traverse from right to left along the north side of the boulder, above the trail.

2. V1
Start on the good foot edge and climb the left side of the north slab of this boulder.

3. V2
The arete.

4. No Fat Chicks V4
Jug start on the left side of the roof. Go straight up.

5. Fat Chicks On Tread Mills V6
Crimp seam from left to right, to the previous problem and up on patina.

6. Lady Fingers V6?
Start on patina crimps at chest height, hard top out. Sit start project.

7. El Bitcho Pantso V1
Splitter crack/lieback up the clean face.

8. 5.9
Sit start the hand to fist crack in the gentle overhang.

9. Thumb In Your Bum V4
Mantle rail on the green face, just right of the micro splitter seam. High mantle.

10. The Watery Grave V3
Start on the flake above the hole under the boulder. Pull to more flakes.

11. Pedaras V2
Start on a left crimp and sloping right pinch.

Eagle Rock

12. Claustrophobia V2 or V5
Sit start on the rail up to the flake and right to the rail for the V2 version. For the V5 version, move left after the flake to the edge and top of the boulder.

13. Confidence Booster V1
Undercling sit start on the large flake. Lieback all the way.

14. Project
Sit start left hand on low crimp, right hand around corner on sloper, then follow rail to top. V3 variation: start on slopers in the middle.

15. God Hates Joel V4
Sit start the flake, then follow it right. Pull hard for the rail on the less than vertical top. V3 if you go up to rounded hold.

16. V2
Start on crimps just left of the seam/flake.

17. Aspen Groove V4
Good edges get you motivated to move right and up along the arete at the edge of the roof. Located just left of the trail.

18. V0
Directly opposite the recess that holds Aspen Groove is a lip traverse warm up.

Eagle Rock

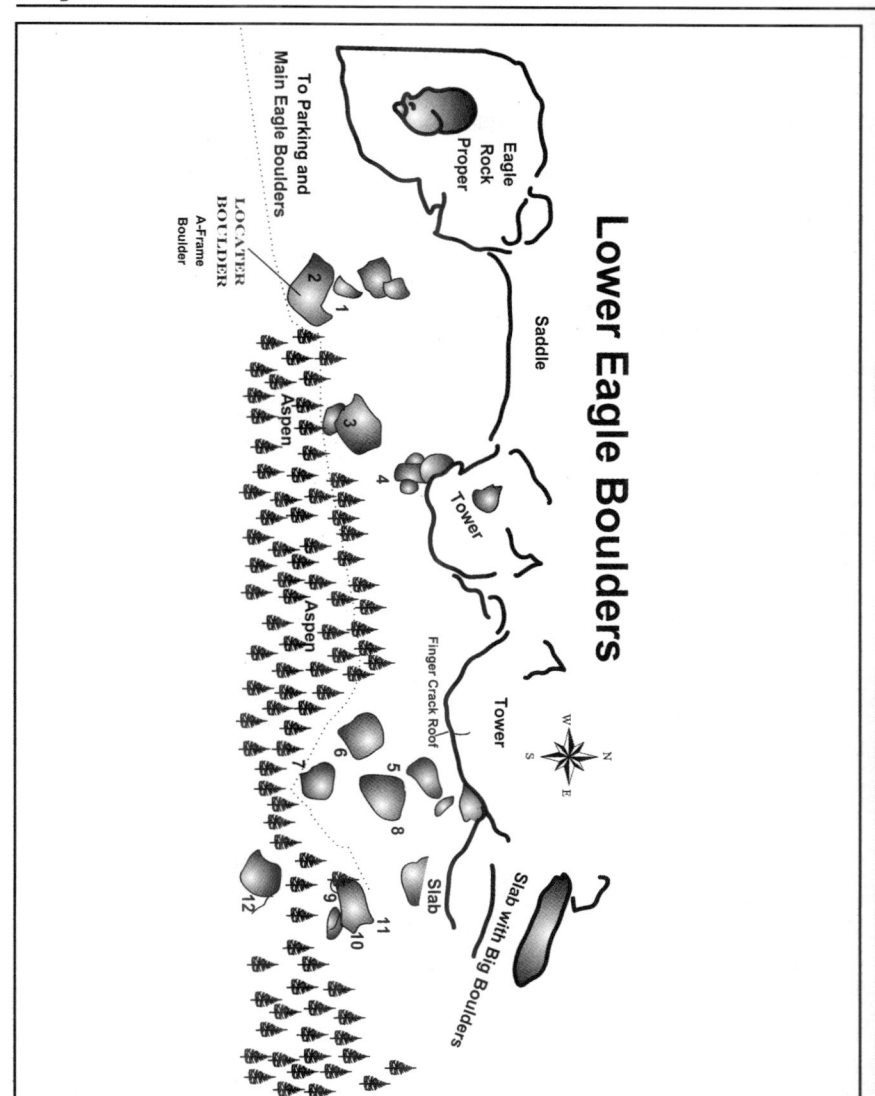

Lower Eagle Boulders

Eagle Rock Proper

Saddle

To Parking and Main Eagle Boulders

LOCATER BOULDER

A-Frame Boulder

Aspen

Aspen

Tower

Tower

Finger Crack Roof

Slab

Slab with Big Boulders

Eagle Rock

175

Lower Eagle Boulders
1. Raisinettes V2/3
Stand start on the gaston left and pinch/undercling right. Pull up the left side of the a-frame. This problem is height dependant.
2. Gist of My Fist V6
Crimpy edges start at eye level on the a-frame's right arete/lip. Move left along the arete/lip and finish at the apex. For the full Gist, start sitting with right hand on sloper and left hand on the obvious edge. Will probably go at around V8.
Warm up slab V0
On the back side of the A Frame boulder is a slab warm up.
3. V3
This problem is on the south side of the huge dark pink boulder. Sit start the problem above the smaller boulder you land on.
4. Rainy Day Blues 5.7
The super good finger to hand splitter crack. Sit start on crimp and sloper to add a grade.
5. Beat It V4
Basketball sloper leads to more slopers over the top.
6. Project
The right leaning seam/sloper edge to slopers at the top.
7. Bag Lady V6
Start on or in the good flake, move left into the vertical flares and finish up.
8. V0
The finger crack that moves up and left.

9. 80 Pounds of Adorable V7

Sit start in the left edge and right mail slot on the middle of the south side of the boulder. Pull to crisp crimp and sloping edges in the seams above. There is a cobble at the lip.

10. Badger Roof V3

Start on crimps just below roof, then pull through the roof. Potential for nasty sit start.

11. Project

The arete on the north side of the boulder.

12. V0 to V2

There are various and good water polished slabs in the aspen trees below the large boulders of the previous 11 problems.

Eagle Rock

Bunker
Tony Gleason and crew.
Photo: Matt Williams

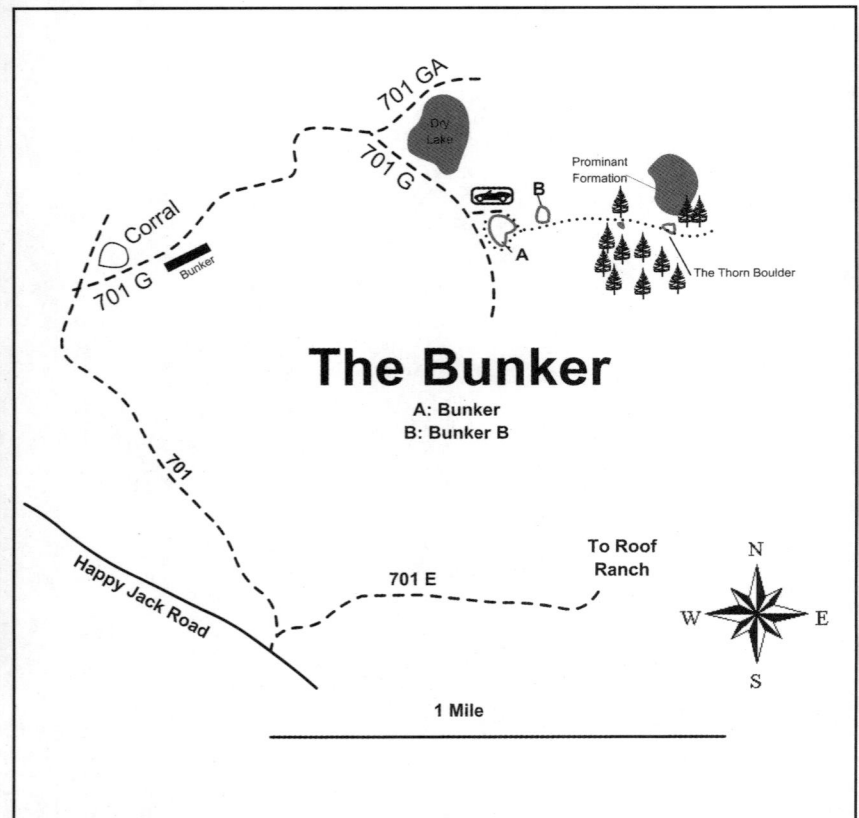

The Bunker

A: Bunker
B: Bunker B

Directions

      7.7 miles down the Happy Jack Highway, at the bottom of a hill with a small creek going under the road, take a left onto road 701. Bear left over the first cattle guard. Follow this road for about a mile and turn right at the corral (701G). Continue down road 701G for a ½ mile until the road forks at a small, usually dry lake. Go right, around the lake, and park at the second band of rocks on the left of the road.

Bunker

	Area Name	Mileage	Turns*
12	Bunker	7.7	4th Left

*From exit 323 turn on to Happy Jack road. Mileage and turns begin when you turn on to Happy Jack Road.

Problem Distribution Table

	V0-V3	V4-V7	V8-V10	V11+	Cracks	Total*
Quantity	25	16	3	0	4	48

*Total includes projects and unrated problems.

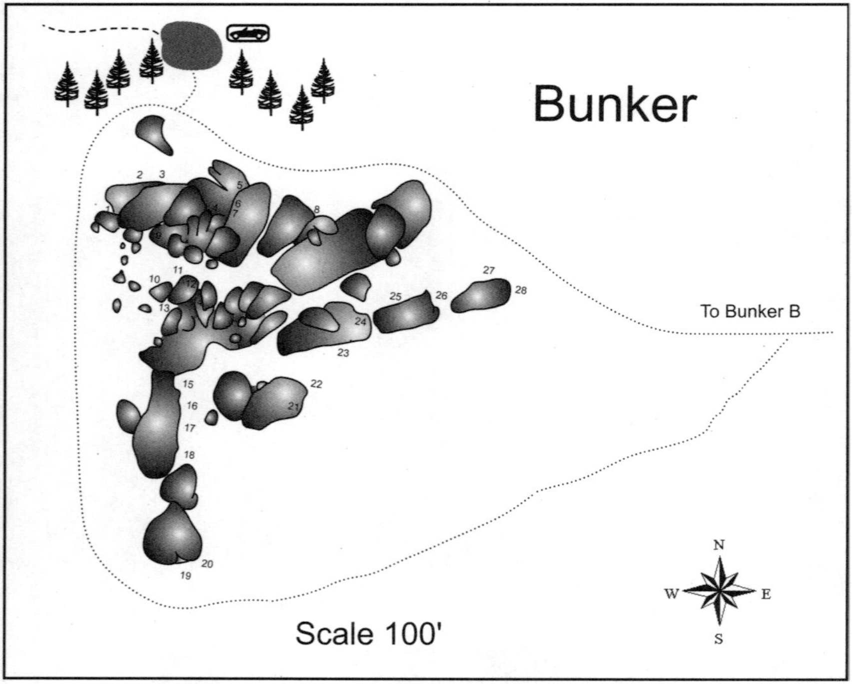
Bunker
1
2 3
4
5
6
7
8
9
10
11
12
13
15
16
17
18
19
20
21
22
23
24
25
26
27
28
To Bunker B
N
W
E
S
Scale 100'

1
2
3

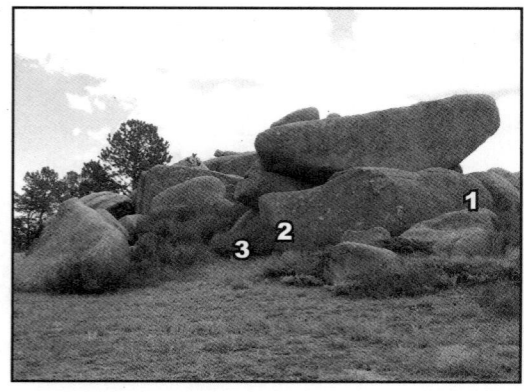

The Bunker

1. Shin and Bones V3
Low start in the A-frame of boulders. Go up the left wall on good edges. Round the arete up top and watch the slippery footholds.

2. V3
Lie back start to the slab.

3. V4
This problem is now overgrown. Use the sloping, open-handed lieback, then toss for the sloping lip of the wall.

4. 5.10
Tall hand and fist crack.

5. V3
This is the arete on your left when looking into the cave. Not much to pull on, but what is there should be enough to do it.

6. Hanibal Lector V7/8
Start low on the lieback flake in the depths of the roof. At the bucket, go left onto crisp edges. The project goes straight out, without using the boulder to the left.

7. Trasher V6
Start low on the lieback flake in the depths of the roof. At the bucket continue out jugs to a chimney top out.

8. V4
Sit start on good holds and go up and left. Straight up is project.

9. The Faith-Based Mantle V4
Small crimps on the undercut slab take you to a big move for the top.

10. V1
Crumbly edges/slopers up the short rock.
11. V1
Arete and slab problem.
12. V2
The left arete/prow on the same boulder as problem 10.
13. 5.11
Overhanging crack where two boulders touch. Roof crack to flared wide crack near top.
14. Back Attack V4
Lie down start the overhanging arete on the top of the big boulder. Half the problem is not sagging to hit the boulder under you. Mantle when you get to the seam.
15. Pocket Rocket V3
Sit start and pull to the eyebrow pocket at mid-height.
16. Welt Kreig Mauer V2
On the right side of the wall, use low edges/side pulls to start. Go up on good, crisp edges.
17. Dream of the Devil V9
Really small opposing crimps up to more small crimps and a flat edge just under the lip. This problem shares a foot with Walt Kreig Mauer.
18. Trouble With Top Outs V3
Thin holds on the left end of the wall, in a small dihedral thing. The top is a bit round.
19. 5.8
The crack on the shot up boulder.

20. It's Only a Small Caliber V1
Use dishes and sloping crimps to go up the bulge. Good warm-up. Thanks to the gun activists, the holds are always changing.

24. In the Groove V3
Sit start the short dihedral hidden in the back of a corridor.
25. The Ghost V3
Climb the crescent shaped seam, which terminates half way up the slab
26. 5.9
The left leaning crack in the hallway.
27. V2
Sit start edges
28. V7
The right leaning, sloping seam located on the end of the boulder.

21. 50 Caliber V2
The slab/mantle problem on shot-out dishes.
22. Bush Breaker V4
Above the bushes, on the rounded bulge of the boulder, go up on bad feet and sloping edges. Use the pinch out right to start.
23. Big Slab V0-V3
Various problems go up the tall slab.

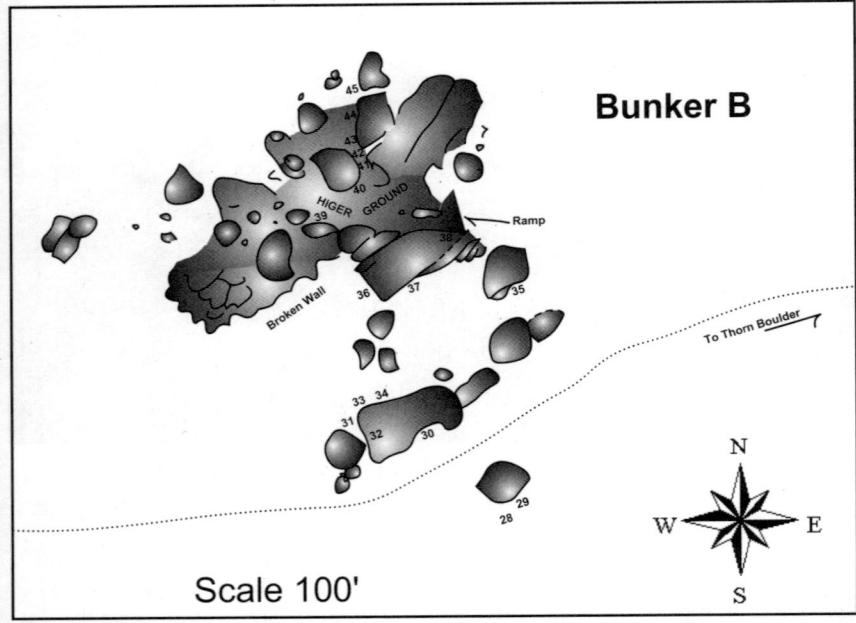

Bunker B

Scale 100'

Bunker B
29. V0-V3
There are several options on the boulder in the field between Bunker B and the field.
30. Project
This shallow dish was worked to near completion but the crux move was never stuck from the start. Low start then iron cross press.
31. Trojan V2
Start this short but good problem with the good foot on the flake and a sloping side pull with the left hand in the dish around the bulge. Go to the top on slopers.

32. French Press V2
Start on a good edge right and move left on the slab. Press up and balance to the top.
33. Nathan's Manly Bulge V8
This is the big undercut bulge at the end of the boulder. Start on slopers on the bulge and power mantle your way up to the good and only edge on top.
34. V2
Undercut slab with a balancey start.
34. High Foot V3
The undercut slab.
35. Achilles Revenge V6/7
Sit start the arete on the smiley face hold, then follow the arete.

Bunker

36. Sugar Cane V1
Seams and edges up the front of the face avoiding the good seam out left.
37. Asha V4
Undercling start this tall, nice face and go for the good incuts above.
38. Weirdo Shit Scoop V4
Edges in the corridor on the way up to the top of the formation.

39. Sausage V4
Lie down start on the good crescent shaped edge. Sticky slopers bring you to the top.

40. Mind Spider V6
Sit start the black inclusion. Slap up on slopers.

41. Sky V2
Low start the crisp edges and crimps.

42. [Chris Sharma's] Muscle Penis V7
Sit start on arete slopers and follow the arete to top.

43. V5
The right most problem on the wall.

44. V3
Moving right following holds is V1. If you move left V3.

45. V4
Sit start and climb prow.

Thorn Boulder

46. Thorn Back V7
Start on the right side of the boulder on crystals and a small, good crimp. Go left to the good edge and continue to the top of the boulder. The original problem starts matched on the good hold and goes at V5.

47. Unter Bissen V2
Sit start on the toothy edge up to the apex of the boulder.

48. Thorn Back Slab V1
The slab on the back of the Thorn Boulder.

Opposite: Nathan Manley gropes at his Manley Bulge.
Photo: Davin Bagdonas

Bunker

Extreme Angles distributes a full line of un-ruly guides. Check out our other titles in your favorite shop or online at

www.ExtremeAngles.com

Do you have a title you'd like us to carry? Do you have a new book idea? If so, contact us. We are looking for new writers!
writers@extremeangles.com

Roof Ranch

Liz Hajek, Brown Eyed Girl
Photo: Josh Helke

Roof Ranch

Roof Ranch Area

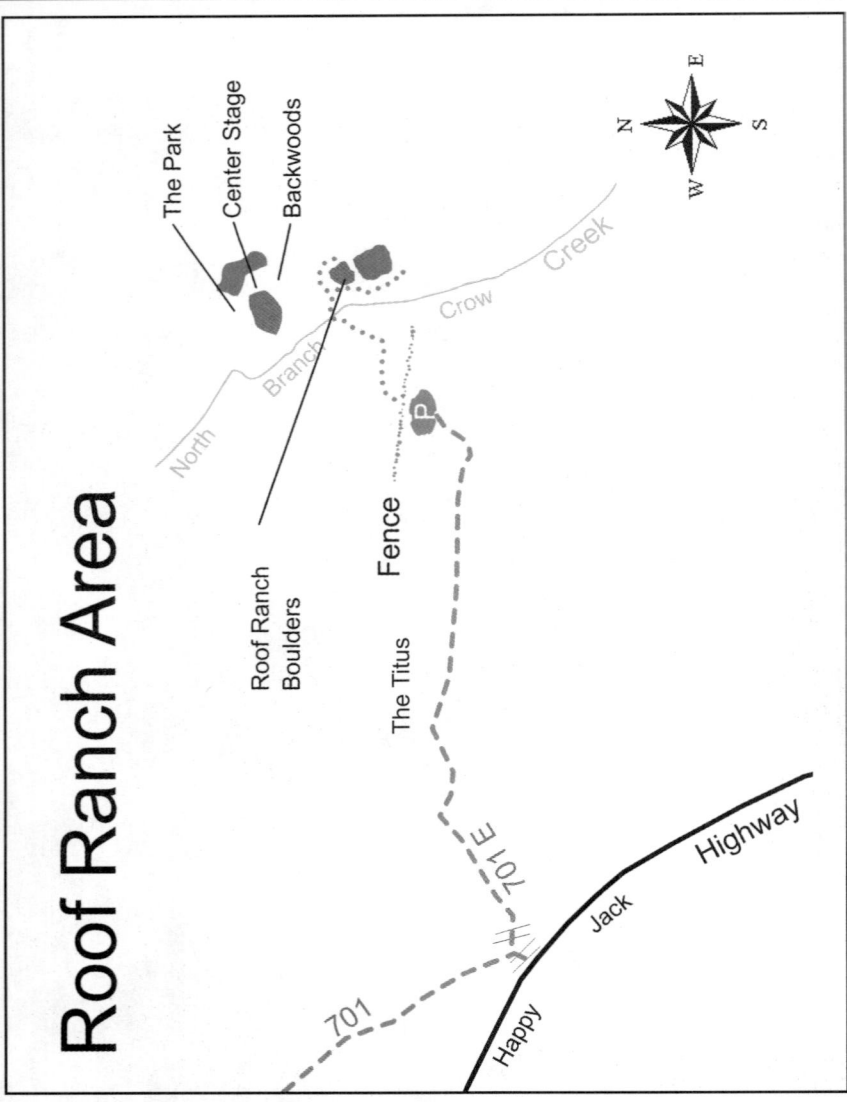

Roof Ranch

	Area Name	Mileage	Turns*
13	Roof Ranch	7.7	4th Left

*From exit 323 turn on to Happy Jack road. Mileage and turns begin when you turn on to Happy Jack Road.

Directions

The Roof Ranch, for ease of description, is divided into five separate areas:The Titus Boulders, The Roof Ranch Boulders, The Back Woods, Center Stage and The Park. All but the Titus Boulders are reached from the same parking area and differ only in location around the central formations of the Roof Ranch. Check the map for where you want to go.

From Interstate 80 and the Happy Jack Exit, take Happy Jack Highway for 7.7 miles. Turn right on Forest Service Road 701.

The Titus Boulders are located along the Forest Service road as you drive in toward the Roof Ranch. Stop just before you get to the loop in the road, around aspens. The Titus Boulders are between the road and the fence.

Problem Distribution Table

	V0-V3	V4-V7	V8-V10	V11+	Cracks	Total*
Quantity	12	11	2	0	6	35

*Total includes projects and unrated problems.

193

Roof Ranch

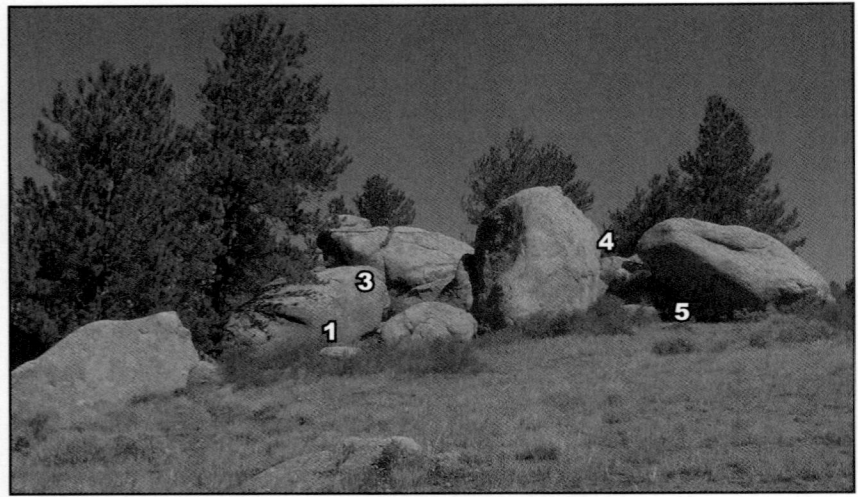

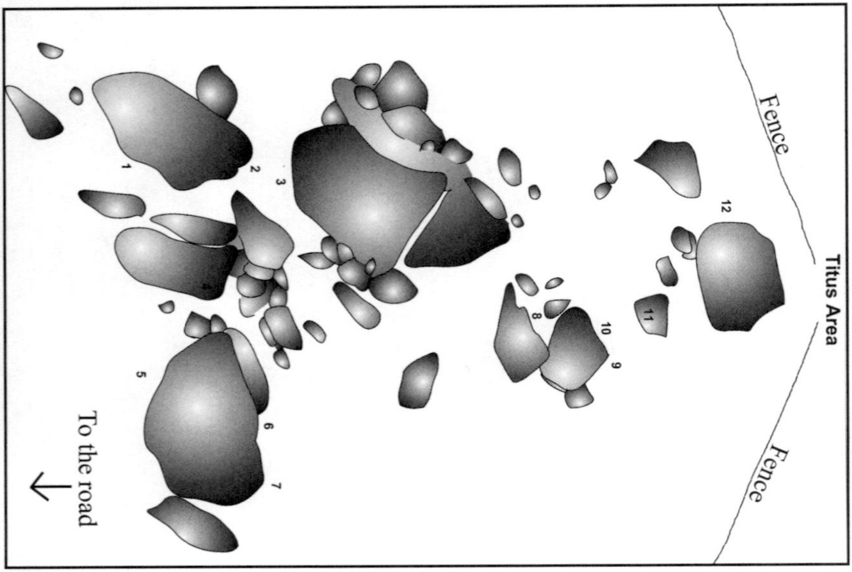
Fence
Fence
Titus Area
To the road
1
2
3
5
6
7
8
9
10
11
12

1
3
4
5

2. Goliath V5

Under a very steep but short roof is a seam and some bad edges. Start on the horizontal seam right of the obvious good hold at the left of the roof. Power up to the lip and mantle. There could be a lower start to this problem...

3. Project V7?

The lieback seam that shuts down up high.

4. V2

Start on the left of the prow and avoid landing in the junk below.

5. Project V?

The big overhanging face with good holds to start on, nothing in the middle, and the lip way up there.

The Titus Boulders

1. David V2

Start this slab/mantle problem with your hands on the lowest of the turtle shell looking texture in the middle of the slabby face. The good holds are not on and are to the right anyway.

Roof Ranch

6. Titus Project
Really tiny crimps up the short wall.
7. Gladiators V3
A really nice problem. Start low on the right leaning seam and when it runs out, rock over the sloping top.
8. Noah V3
Sit start this short problem on the lowest seam and pull straight up to board the ship.
9. The Electric Mexican V4
Slap up the prow using the vertical seam on the left side and the texture on the right.
10. Project?
The sloper-covered face.
11. V0
A good warm up on slabby liebacks.
12. Paul V5
A mantle problem. Start on the low, sloping middle of the face by sitting on a bush. Mantle to a good edge.

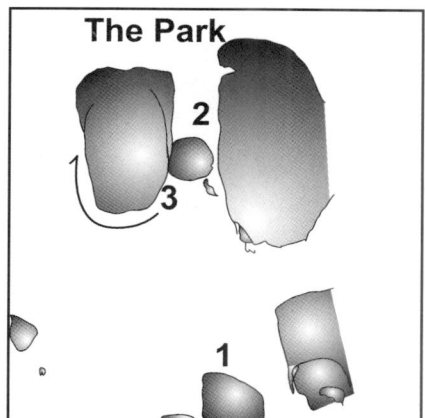

The Park

1. V4
Go up the steep, leaning seams.
2. Skinny Minny V7
Very small undercling to small crimps over the bulge.
3. A Walk in the Park Project
The horizontal crack that splits the large boulder, from right to left, down around then up.

The Back Woods

1. V2
Start on the edge in a seam of sorts and climb left, following the left leaning flake.

2. V3
Same start as the previous problem, but goes up right and finishes on the bulge.

3. V2
Edges up the left face of the west face of the boulder.

4. Golden Waterfall V5
Sit start and use slopers and crimps up the diagonal seams to the top.

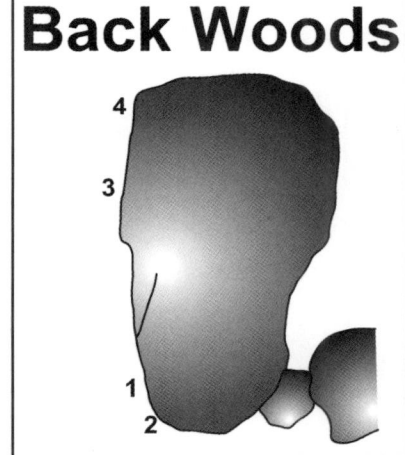

Back Woods

Opposite: Liz Hajek, Golden Waterfall
Photo: Josh Helke

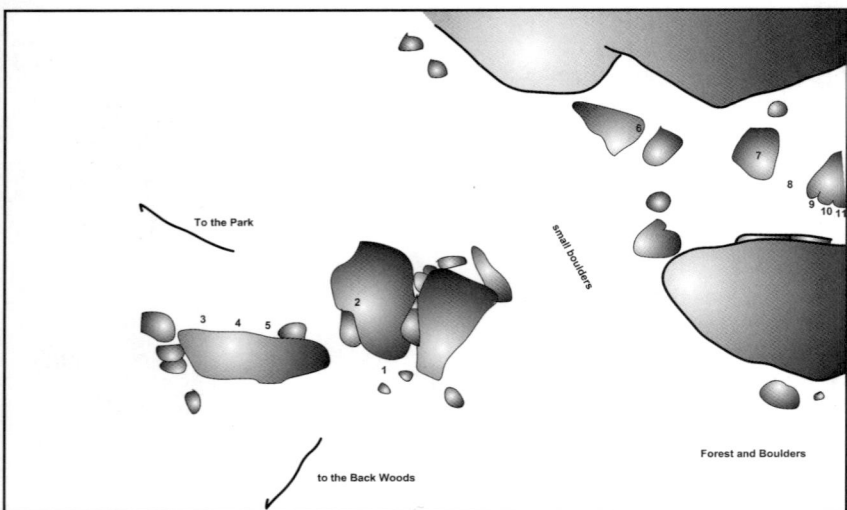

Center Stage

1. Brown Eyed Girl V4, V5, and V7
Stacked seams up the south facing prow of a down sloping boulder. Campus start on the lowest seam and go straight up. The right variation after the start is V5 while the left variation is V7.

2. A Week After Me V3
Horizontal seam to a vertical seam.

3. Pour les Cons V5
A very small right hand crimp and a jump to a slopey left hand start. Go up on nice horizontal seams. The static start from the bad right crimp is hard.

4. V8
Start under roof, climb the arete and top out by the 1 foot high tree.

5. Reach Out V8
Reach out with the right hand when standing on a good rail and prepare for a shoulder-ripping strain. Stack a pad and jump start if you're of average height.

6. V0
The right leaning, left, knife edge arete of the big triangular boulder.

7. 5.8
A splitter fist crack to wider that faces east.

8. 5.10b
A perfect finger crack that starts at shoulder level and faces west.

9. 5.11a
The left crack on the overhanging south face of the tall boulder.

10. 5.10d
The right crack on the overhanging south face of the boulder.

11. V2
Climb the arete.

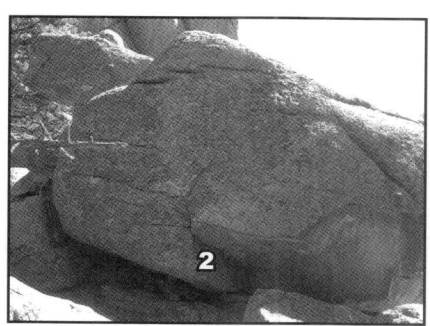

**Following pages: Problem 6, V0
Photo: Matt Williams**

Roof Ranch

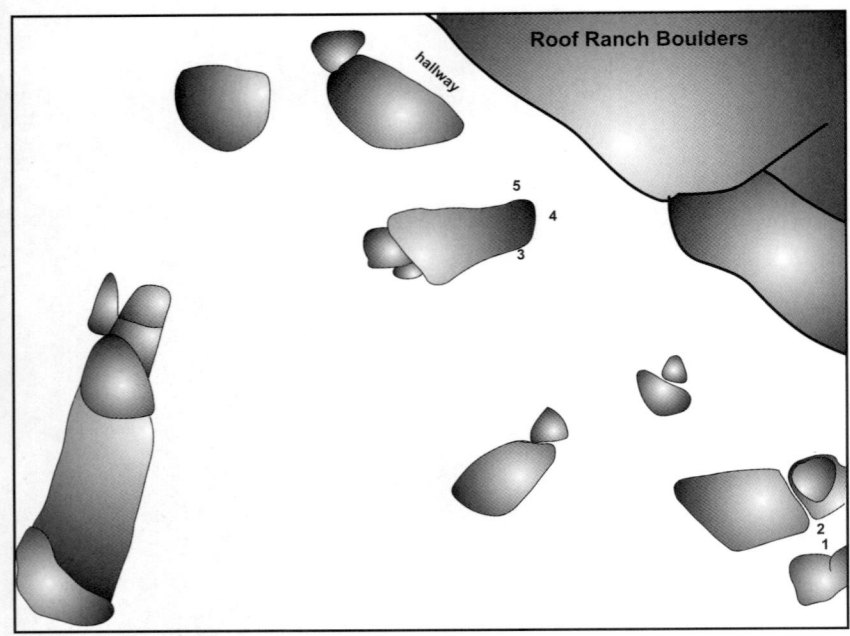

Roof Ranch Boulders
1. 5.10a
The left leaning hand crack and thin-ner that faces north and has a log below it.
2. 5.11d
Sit start as far back as possible in the wide crack/squeeze chimney roof.
3. Remnant Militia V6
Sit start this problem and finish up the arete on sharp crimps.
4. V4
The prow of the boulder.
5. V5
Crimps to the top.

roof ranch

Campjack Rocks

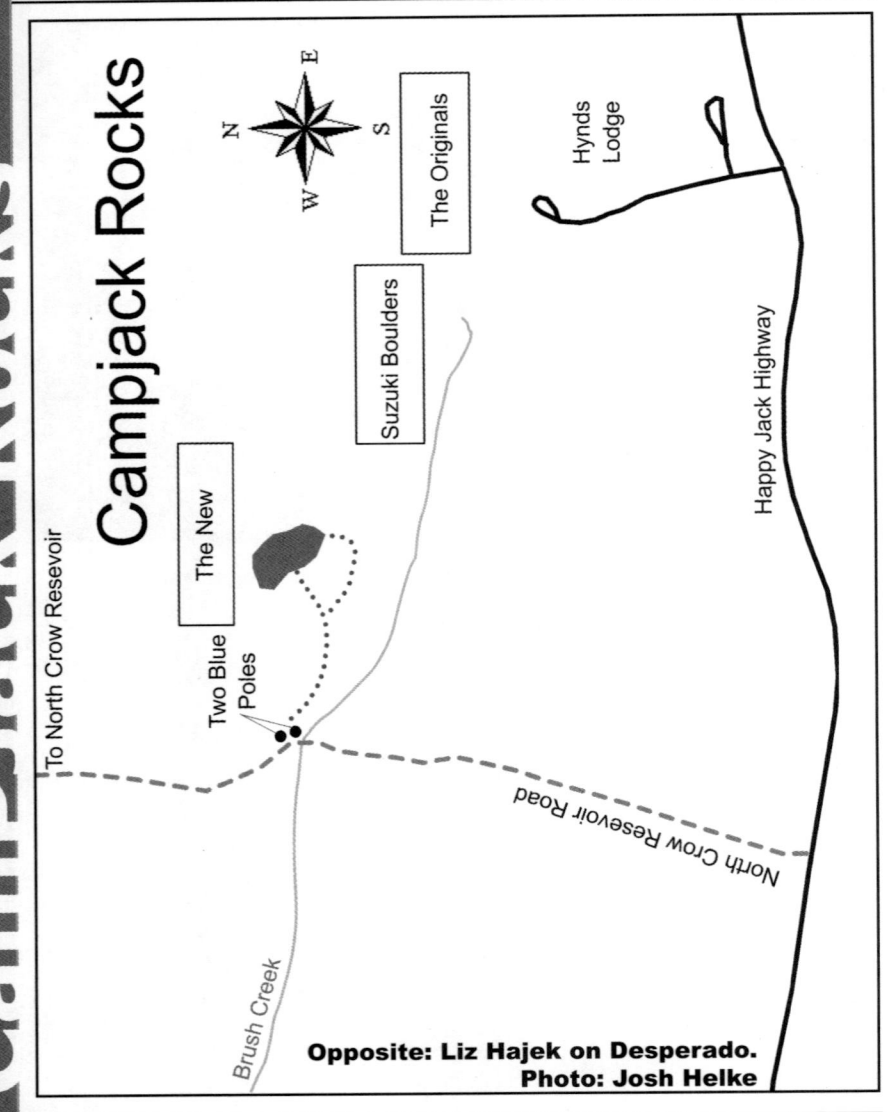

To North Crow Resevoir

Campjack Rocks

N E S W

The Originals

Suzuki Boulders

The New

Hynds Lodge

Happy Jack Highway

Two Blue Poles

North Crow Resevoir Road

Brush Creek

**Opposite: Liz Hajek on Desperado.
Photo: Josh Helke**

Campjack Rocks

	Area Name	Mileage	Turns*
14	Campjack Rocks	12	7th Left

*From exit 323 turn on to Happy Jack road. Mileage and turns begin when you turn on to Happy Jack Road.

Directions

Take the Happy Jack Highway 12 miles and turn left on North Crow Reservoir Road. Continue for about a mile and park next to two blue poles on the right. Follow the trail along the creek to access the climbing.

Problem Distribution Table

	V0-V3	V4-V7	V8-V10	V11+	Cracks	Total*
Quantity	18	11	3	0	1	40

*Total includes projects and unrated problems.

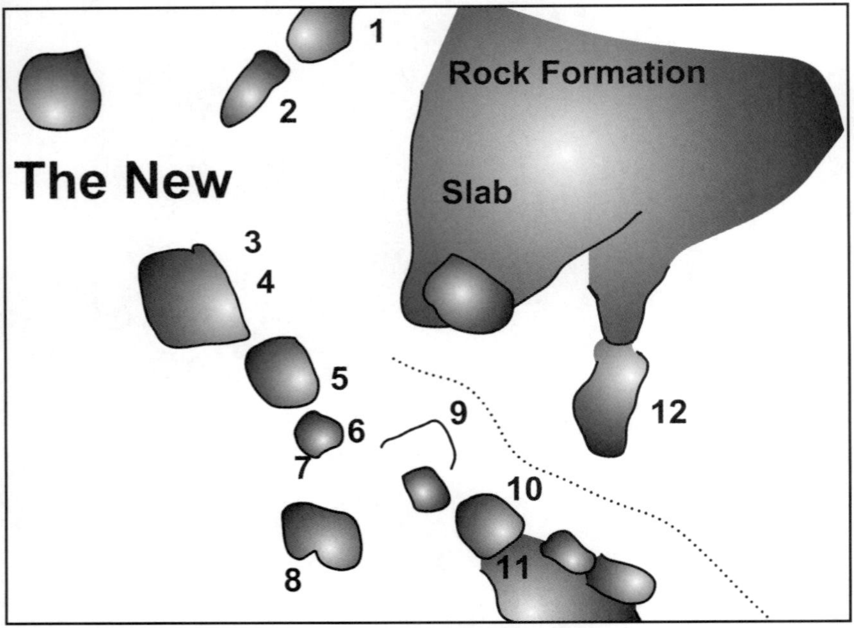
Rock Formation
The New
Slab
1
2
3
4
5
6
7
8
9
10
11
12

The New

1. Project

Crimps up the face on the right side of the alcove up the left side of the gully.

2. Superficial Man V5/6

A really short problem. Sit start on the crescent shaped crisp edge and go for the sloping lip.

3. Scottrope V?

Same start as Skeavy Bastards. Move from a crack to crimps in the middle of the face to the sloping lip out right. A reach for Blunk.

1

Campjack Rocks

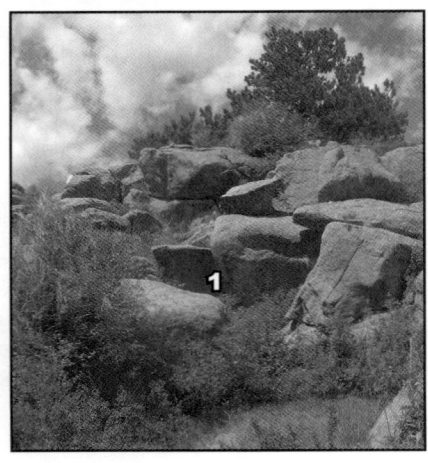

4. Skeavy Bastards V4
Sit start on good holds, move left and up along the seam then straight up to the vertical seam at the lip.

5. V4
A good foot and balance will get you started on this steep slab.

6. V3
Sit start on sharp, crisp crimps and go up for more.

7. Emu Dreamer V4
Good jug to bad edges. The start is undercut.

Campjack Rocks

8. Unnamed V0-V3
Down in the aspen grove is a wall to warm up on with several varieties of problems. The left most is a good V3.

9. Desparado V9
Low start on good in-cut crimps at the back of the roof. Big move to the in-cuts in the roof farther out and finish right.

10. V1
Sit start the good edges and pull straight up.

11. Project
Start on horrible small holds and move left into worse. A really hard line.

12. Apostrophe V8
Sit start left hand crimp with your right hand on the undercling and top out on slopers.

Tony
Gleason on Sweet
Sweet Lovin'
Photo: Davin
Bagdonas

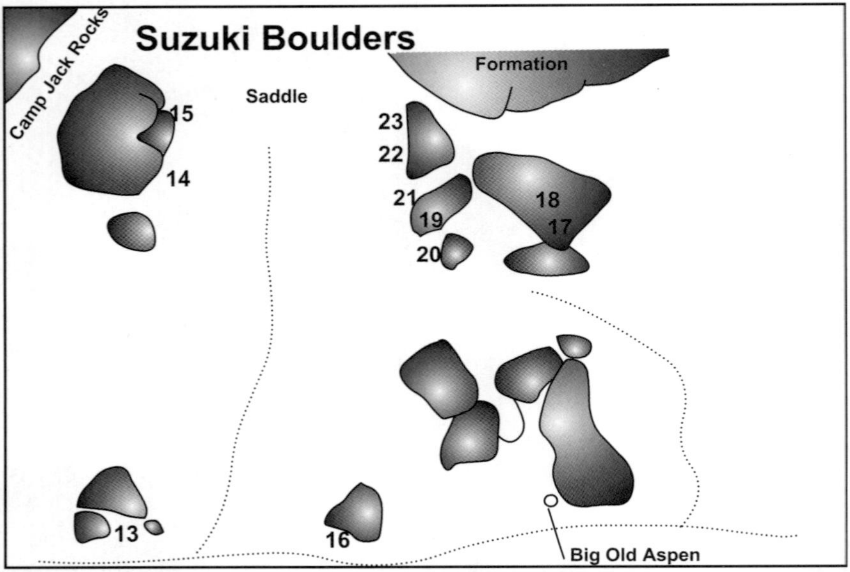

Suzuki Boulders

Formation

Saddle

Camp Jack Rocks

15

14

23

22

21

19

18

17

20

13

16

Big Old Aspen

Suzuki Boulders

13. Glitterali V3
The diagonal undercling on the white face along the trail is where you start.

14. Project
Just left of the previous project is a very flaring crack that starts in the cave. Negotiate the horrible moves out the roof to the flared crack above. This is an old Bob Scarpelli project.

15. Project
The long off fingers/tight hands roof crack above the shelf and bush. This is an old Hidetaka Suzuki project.

16. V1
The dish of the slab along the trail.

17. Suzuki Roof Linkup V6
Start down and right of the good

13

seam for the Suzuki Roof. It's a long way to the goods.

18. Suzuki Roof V4
This is a really cool looking roof that goes at a reasonable grade. Start on the lowest end of the good seam and go all the way out to the lip. Pull the crux to get on top.

19. Turd Farmer V2/3
This is on the boulder to the left of the Suzuki Roof. Sit start on good edges on the right end of the face with turds under it. Up on good slopeing edges.

20. Turd Farmer Traverse V5
Start on the good edges of the left end of the boulder and climb out right to the previous problem where you finish.

The next three problems are behind the Suzuki Boulder.

21. V4
Short roof using a crack to the lip.

22. V3
Slopers to the lip.

23. Unnamed V2
Arete traverse.

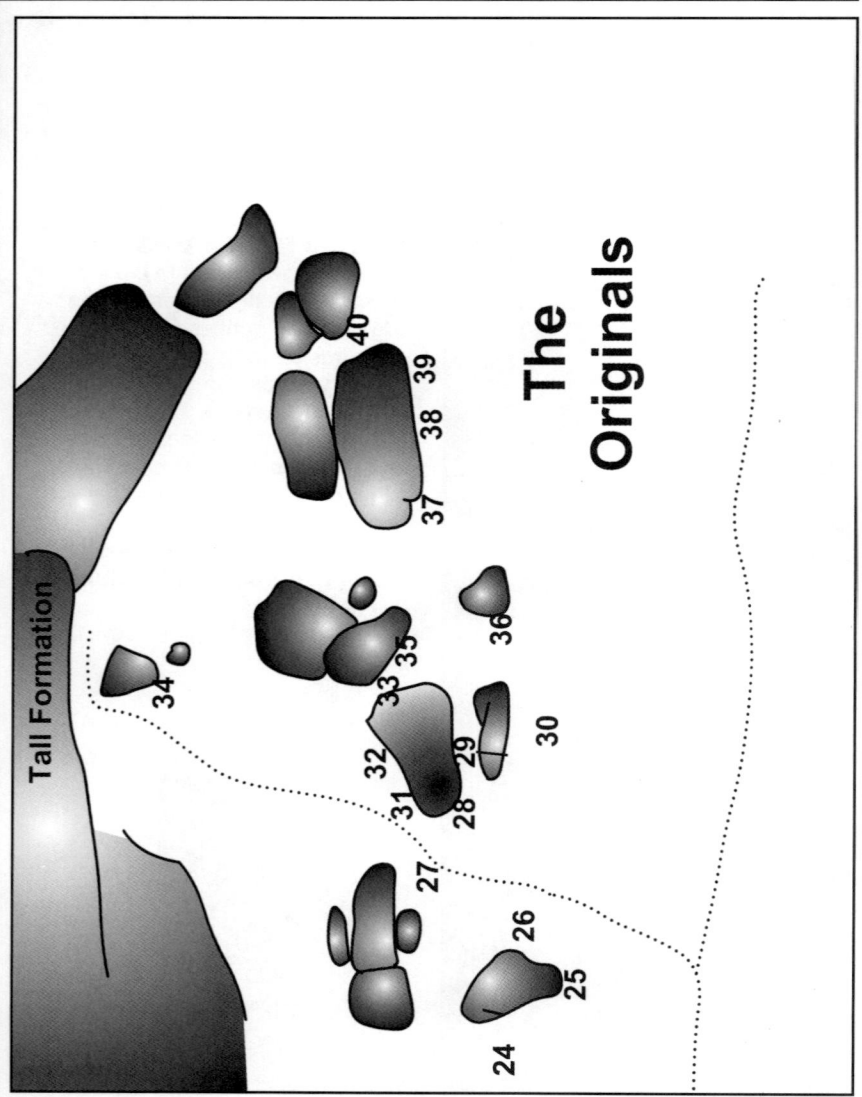

The Originals
24. 5.10c
The finger crack on good jams. Sit start.
25. Little America V5
Start under the totally blank roof. Go out with a big move to the flake and up and left after the flake. V6 sit start low left in crack traverse lip of roof into Little America.
26. V0-
Tall, low angle slab.
27. Sweet Sweet Lovin' V1
Low good rail to high good rail and the top. Nice long pulls.
28. V1
Jump start to the sticky sloping lip of the bulge.

29. Joy Ride V0
Start on the low good edge of the boulder. Slap along the sloping lip and mantle at the flake above the lip or continue all the way around to the apex of the boulder for a V1.
30. Bitch V2
Uncomfortable start in the shallow open book. Up to good edges just under the top of the rock.
31. Project
The left leaning sloping edge that's barely there. Bad feet.
32. V3
Start on the ledge and do a big move to the lip of the gentle overhang. A very weird mantle/hump move gets you to the goodness.
33. Militant Poetry V5
Just across from 35. Start on right

leaning seam, then slap up and right on slopers.

34. Lonesome Dove V8
Start on the lowest end of the boulder on the obvious low edges. Big move to the sloper and you've got it.

35. V1
The slab where it climbs like a V1 slab.

36. Loaf V2
Cruxy low start with a good foot. Move toward the loaf inclusion just out of reach.

37. Ra Slab Left V1
The flake and slab on the left side of the nice slab.

38. Ra Slab Right V0
Patina up the right side of the nice slab.

39.
Low start on bad crimpy things to the grainy sloper, mantle onto the slab then up. It's the problem on the right side of the actual slab.

40. Project
Sit start crimps to more crimps and few more crimps. It looks like there might be more crimps up higher too. This starts on the far right side of the Ra Slab in the corridor, but it is not a slab.

Campjack Rocks

Index Of Named Boulder Problems

Symbols

Bret Hull on Sweet Sweet Lovin'
Photo: Davin Bagdonas

More from Extreme Angles

Fat Crack Country: Rock Climbing in Vedauwoo
By Zach Orenczak $19.95

The most comprehensive climbing guide to Vedauwoo. Details the colorful history with bizarre anecdotes on the wild characters that established some of Vedauwoo's most classic lines

Vedauwoo Bouldering
By Davin Bagdonas $19.95

Over 560 boulder problems are covered in the long awaited *Vedauwoo Bouldering.* Detailed maps and photographs as well as descriptions give boulderers three ways to find a problem. With so many problems and near perfect landings, Vedauwoo is the perfect destination for boulderers of any level.

Free Climbs of Devils Tower 15th edition
By Dingus McGee and the Last Pioneer Woman
$ 9.95

Written by the legendary Dingus McGee who pioneered some of the Tower's sickest and most classic lines. His familiarity with the rock and the climbs is conveyed in concise topo-style diagrams displaying all the information you need to get safely on and off the tower.

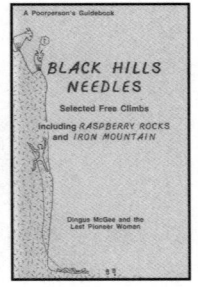

Black Hills Needles: Selected Free Climbs
By Dingus McGee and the Last Pioneer Woman
$9.95

Including over 300 high quality accessible routes, *Black Hills Needles,* is for those that have the Needles on their map. Jam packed with maps, odd diagrams and wacky illustrations, this guide is perfect for those seeking a wit of history.